THE ATHEIST
DEBATER'S
HANDBOOK

THE ATHEIST DEBATER'S HANDBOOK

by B. C. Johnson

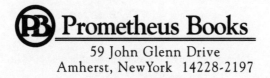

Prometheus Books

59 John Glenn Drive
Amherst, New York 14228-2197

Published 1983 by Prometheus Books
59 John Glenn Drive, Amherst, New York 14228-2197,
716-691-0133. FAX: 716-691-0137.

Library of Congress Catalogue Number: 81-80487
ISBN 0-87975-210-6

Printed in the United States of America on acid-free paper.

I gratefully acknowledge the critical suggestions of Mr. Steven L. Mitchell, Assistant Editor of Prometheus Books, whose valuable assistance has resulted in a more cogent manuscript.

Contents

Preface

Much has been written in an effort to resolve the debate over whether belief in God can be rationally defended. However, pointing to the volumes contributed by theologians, philosophers, and lay persons is no reason to conclude that nothing further can be said concerning this vital question. Scholarly journals continue to publish new arguments and discussions focusing on issues that surround God's existence. Indeed, there are three journals devoted exclusively to the treatment of questions and topics in the philosophy of religion. Because they are generally found in university libraries, publications of this type are, for the most part, inaccessible to the public. Even if these journals were readily available, the articles they contain are nonetheless quite long, complicated, and rough-going; few people have the time, persistence, or stamina to wade through them.

This handbook is, in part, an attempt to summarize the

best arguments from these journals, and to offer a concise set of rejoinders for use by atheists in their formal (and informal) debates with theists. Older, more traditional, arguments are included as well, but these are treated in greater detail than ever before. Here and there I have set forth original arguments which I hope will advance the debate if only slightly. Great care has been taken to insure that digressions and rhetoric are minimized. The result is a short book, yet one that contains an unrelenting presentation of argument and analysis.

For some time now atheists have been in need of firm grounds upon which to base their position. My handbook offers them this foundation. Some will look upon my efforts as a sinister attempt to further undermine social values. Actually, my purpose is to show that atheism is an intellectually respectable viewpoint despite recent efforts to prove otherwise.

One point should be made concerning the structure of this handbook. In scholarly works there are numerous quotations and references which serve as important study aides. This technique seems inappropriate for a layman's handbook. The value of this work is found in its simplicity. For this reason the text is not interrupted by quotes or references. Where necessary credit has been given in footnotes and in an extensive bibliography.

THE ATHEIST
DEBATER'S
HANDBOOK

I. God and Atheism

Theists believe in God, while atheists do not have such a belief. Many theists insist that it is the responsibility of the atheist to offer evidence justifying his lack of belief in God. But is the theist's demand rational? Must the atheist justify his lack of belief in God? Or does the burden rest with the theist?

Both the theist and the atheist agree on many points. For example, they share a belief in the existence of a physical universe composed of orderly atomic structures, and they may even hold very similar moral beliefs. However, the theist asserts that a *further* belief is necessary in order to explain both the existence and the characteristics of those things about which he and the atheist have similar beliefs.

The first point to notice is that the theist has proposed to explain a set of facts. Now if one offers an explanation of something, one must be prepared to provide reasons for accepting the explanation. Consider what would happen if justifications were not required for all proposed explanations. We could "explain" something in whatever manner suited our whim. We could assert, for instance, that the earth turns because muscular ghosts push it. It might be claimed that the wind blows because air spirits are fanning themselves. We could even offer incompatible explanations of the same facts and there would be no way to decide among them. The atheist is like a man who does not necessarily claim to know what makes the earth turn but who nevertheless does not believe that muscular ghosts push it. It is vital for the one who believes in such muscular ghosts to offer reasons for his belief. By the same token, it is incumbent upon the theist to provide reasons for his belief that God is the true explanation of the universe and morality. The atheist, for his part, does not necessarily offer an explanation; he simply does not accept the theist's explanation. Therefore, the atheist need only demonstrate that the theist has failed to justify *his* position.

Another point to note is that the atheist believes in the existence of the universe and does not believe in anything which is more fundamental. The theist believes in the existence of the universe and — in addition — he believes in the existence of God. The theist, therefore, believes in one more thing than the atheist. If all beliefs should be justified, then surely the more one believes, the more justification one must produce. Clearly, the theist must justify this extra belief to the atheist. If, on the other hand, beliefs need *not* be justified, then we might as well give in to pure anarchy and admit that rational discussion is impossible.

Consider the following example illustrating why a justification for such additional beliefs is required: Suppose there is a lawsuit in which I claim that a written contract exists while the other party to the alleged contract denies it. When challenged to prove the existence of such a contract I claim that it is up to my opponent to prove that it does not exist. Obviously, no case is ever conducted in this way. The person who believes in the existence of the contract possesses at least one more belief than he who denies its existence. Courts demand some justification for such extra beliefs, otherwise no case could ever be resolved.

As a further illustration, suppose I accuse someone of breaking my car window. This person denies the charge and demands to know the nature of the evidence pointing to him as the culprit. I reply that it is his responsibility to produce evidence indicating that he did *not* break the window. I believe in one more thing than he does: that he broke the window. Plainly I must first justify this extra belief. Until I do so, the accused person need not support his denial. And when he finally does support it, he need only do so by finding flaws in the evidence I have advanced against him.

Imagine that I just claimed there to be a gigantic man-eating frog in the local lake, and a friend denies it. It would be incumbent upon me to prove that such a thing exists, and not my friend's responsibility to disprove it.

Suppose I am a physicist and I claim to have discovered a new form of matter. My colleagues deny the discovery. I must produce evidence to support the discovery. They need not produce evidence to suggest that I have discovered nothing.

In each of these examples I have claimed to possess a belief which someone else has denied. I have expressed my belief in one more thing than can be found in his list of beliefs. I must justify this additional belief. He need not justify his denial. The reason for this procedure is fairly straightforward: requests for disproof lead to hopeless situations. If I claim that a contract exists and demand that the skeptic prove me wrong, he could claim that there is evidence to disprove my claim but that it is up to me to disprove the existence of *that* evidence. I in turn could claim that there is evidence discrediting his evidence but that it is now his job to disprove the existence of *my* evidence. And so it would go without end. Once the demand for disproof is permitted to go unchallenged, it becomes impossible to prove any claim. Much time would be wasted in futile attempts to undermine evidence only to find more of the same piled up in its place.

How does this reasoning work when applied to the controversy separating theists and atheists? The theist claims that the atheist must disprove God's existence. The atheist could reply that there is conclusive evidence to suggest that God does not exist and thus it is the theist who must disprove the existence of such evidence. The demand for disproof inevitably leads to an inconclusive farce. The demand for proof, on the other hand, can have conclusive results. Therefore, the only sensible procedure would be to demand proof, not disproof.

If additional beliefs are held, one must be prepared to justify them in light of statements to the contrary. If, on the other hand, a person does not possess additional beliefs, then his position must prevail provided that his opponent is unable to offer good reasons for him to abandon it. The atheistic position must prevail if the theist is unable to support his belief in the existence of God.

Atheism can be more positively defended in the following way.[1] We can properly claim to know that many things are not so if reasons have not been offered to support the claim that they are so. For example, I am able to claim that I know my friend Frank is not at home precisely because there is no reason to believe that he is at home. There is no noise coming from his house, the lights are out at a time when he is usually awake, his bed is empty, and so forth. Everything seems to count for my belief and nothing against it. I could discover that I was mistaken, but the possibility of error exists for virtually any knowledge claim one might make.

The parallel between the belief that Frank is at home and the belief that God exists is an exact one. If Frank is at home, there will be evidence indicating this state of affairs. On the other hand, if there is no evidence that he is at home, one can claim to know he is not at home. Similarly, if God exists, there will be evidence of this; signs will emerge which point to such a conclusion. However, if there is no evidence that He exists, then one can claim to know that God does not exist. It could be claimed that God exists but has simply left no evidence upon which to base the claim. But such a statement would be much like saying that Frank is at home yet there is no evidence of his presence. Neither claim seems plausible. Frank is normally involved with his house in various ways and if there is no evidence of involvement, one can assume that he is not at home. Presumably, God is even more involved with the world than Frank is with his house—after all, God created and designed the world. Therefore, if the evidence of God's involvement with the world is no more compelling than that of Frank's present involvement with his house, then one is equally justified in claiming that God does not exist as one is in claiming that Frank is not at home.

If I am correct, then the claim that there is no God can be justified on the grounds that there is no reason to believe that he exists. What has just been said is no more surprising than if I were to claim to know that there is no Santa Claus because there is no reason to believe in him.

Are there reasons to believe in God's existence? This question will occupy us during much of the remainder of this book.

II. God and Science

There is a tendency among theists to offer, as evidence for the existence of God, phenomena which "science cannot explain." For example, neo-Darwinism has thus far been unsuccessful in explaining the development of the turtle's shell. All conclusions have been based upon the gradual modification of the rib-cage of its ancestors. Intermediate structures between rib-cage and shell would have had no use and therefore would not have been favored by natural selection. God, the theist claims, must therefore be the explanation of the turtle's shell.

God certainly could be used to explain puzzling phenomena. However, the issue is not whether a particular explanation can be provided but, instead, whether the explanation presented is in fact correct.

To illustrate this point, let us consider the tendency of water to form into drops. One could explain this phenomenon by conjuring up invisible fairies who deliberately isolate a small amount of water and exert pressure around it to keep it in the shape of a drop. This fairy-theory would adequately explain the tendency of water to form into drops. But would it be the *correct* explanation? Suppose that, as a matter of fact, no other explanation is known. Would this information alone make the fairy explanation correct?

The theist uses just this type of argument to make his case. He contends that since God is an *adequate* explanation of a puzzling phenomenon, and no other adequate explanation is known, then God must be the correct explanation. Two problems exist when this approach is employed. First, an adequate explanation is not likely to be the correct explanation merely because it is adequate. Other explanations might be developed which are equally adequate. For example, a man might drown accidentally as the result of a bad fall or because a murderer had held him under water. Both explanations of the drowning would be adequate. But only one would be correct. The adequacy of an explanation is no guarantee of its correctness. Adequacy is not the only mark of a correct explanation. An explanation must be adequate in order to be correct, but adequacy alone is not sufficient.

Nor is an adequate explanation more likely to be the correct explanation merely because it is the *only* adequate explanation we know. This is apparent from the fact that we now know the correct explanations of many things which could at one time have been explained only by invoking the *direct* action of God or a spirit. For example, primitive man had no idea that fire consisted of energy released by rapid oxidation of carbon compounds. He had no knowledge of chemistry at all. However, he might have theorized that fire was a miraculous generation of heat and light caused directly by God. If the God explanation is adequate, then at some earlier time this was the only adequate explanation known to us. Examples such as this can be multiplied indefinitely. If "the only known adequate explanation" has so often been the incorrect explanation, it can hardly be claimed that "the only known adequate explanation" is likely to be the correct one merely *because* it is the only adequate explanation we know. As an historical fact, we have usually decided that a particular explanation is correct only when compared to several competing alternative explanations which are also adequate. Since the theist must concede that the direct action of God is an adequate explanation, then at least one alternate explanation has always been available.

An explanation is not shown to be correct merely because it is adequate. Nor is it shown to be correct because it is the only adequate explanation we have yet developed. An explanation is shown to be correct when experiments designed to disconfirm it fail. These falsifying experiments must be coupled with confirming experiments. But how are we to determine whether God can be used to correctly explain anything? We cannot see Him in action and no experiment — whether of the confirming or disconfirming type — reveals Him. Theists rely completely on God as the only adequate explanation known thus far. But this, as we have seen, does not imply that God is the correct explanation. Unless God can be established as *the* correct explanation, we can justly regard the theistic point of view as only one *possible* adequate explanation.

Science searches for *correct* explanations and does not settle for merely known or adequate ones. If science had been content to explain every puzzling phenomenon by saying that God caused it, there would have been no scientific progress whatsoever. Just imagine the knowledge science would have accumulated by now if it had taken that route. All scientific knowledge would consist of one thing: God. No electrons, atoms or molecules would be invoked as explanations. What causes fire to burn? God. What causes lightning? God. What causes rain? God. The success of science in developing correct explanations has been based solely on its refusal to take the easy way out and proclaim God as the explanation.[2] And the success of science in developing correct explanations is reason enough to believe that such a refusal is justified. Consistent discovery of the truth is the best justification of procedures for discovering truth. (Remember we are discussing the explanation of such things as the causes of lightning and the turtle's shell. The explanation of orderly interactions among the basic materials of the universe will be discussed in the following section on "God and the Laws of Nature.")

Since primitive times, great scientific progress has been made. We have developed explanations, based upon natural causes, for many events previously left unexplained. How, then, can we know that a presently unexplained phenomenon will not turn out to have some natural explanation? The total class of unexplained events is not necessarily the same as that group which is unexplainable within the arena of natural causes. If it were the same, no scientific progress would ever have been made. This is so because scientific progress by definition consists of developing natural explanations for phenomena previously unexplained in these terms. To claim that there are phenomena which must be considered unexplainable is to predict what the future course of scientific investigation will or will not reveal. And this would be mere guesswork.

The theist may object that quite often we can accurately

predict what will be considered true. For example, if in a murder case no evidence turns up to vindicate the accused, we have good reason to suspect that no such evidence exists. But the example above is based upon familiar situations in which we have previous experience to let us know what to expect. However, when we consider the future course of scientific investigation, experience can only lead us to expect the unexpected. Science has produced many unexpected discoveries throughout its history.

That we are at present ignorant about an explanation of some particular phenomenon cannot be the basis for distinguishing between what is unexplainable and that which is unexplained. Present ignorance is common to both possibilities. We would be no more ignorant at present if a phenomenon were unexplainable than we would be if it were merely unexplained. In neither case would we have an explanation. We can say that we know of no natural explanation but that there probably is one. Or we can say that we know of no natural explanation and there probably is *not* one. Present ignorance is compatible with—indeed, included in—both statements. If present ignorance is compatible with both statements, then present ignorance cannot be used as an argument against either of them.

If the theist is to use our present ignorance of an explanation grounded in natural causes as an argument for God's existence, then he must also grant present ignorance of the existence of God. For the existence of God is precisely the conclusion which the argument set out to prove. There would be no point in providing such an argument if we already granted the existence of God. Therefore, if we use present ignorance as a premise in an argument for God's existence, this ignorance must be ignorance of any possible natural causes *and* of the existence of God. After all, just as God's existence cannot be established by merely assuming that he exists, in like manner the validity of an explanation grounded in natural causes cannot be established by assuming its applicability. An argument must be based upon assumptions which are not disputed, otherwise its conclusion is disputable and the argument will have settled nothing. For this reason, an argument's conclusion ought not to be included among its list of assumptions.

Bearing in mind the above point, the use of present ignorant as an argument for God's existence will result in self-contradiction. Let us backtrack for a moment to consider how the turtle-shell argument really performs. The theist argues: "What is the origin of the turtle's shell? I don't know. You don't know. Therefore God originated the turtle's shell." This is really saying: "What is the origin of the turtle's shell? I don't know. You don't know. Therefore we *both* know—that is, we know that God originated it." An honest person, when confronted with something he knows nothing about, will admit he knows nothing about it. To argue that we do *not* know how a thing was brought about is clearly not to argue that we *know something* concerning how it was brought about. Ignorance implies only ignorance. If we begin the argument from science by assuming a position of ignorance as to the existence of adequate natural causes and the existence of God, then we cannot proceed to the conclusion that God exists. The argument can move only from ignorance to ignorance. It can conclude that God exists only if it begins with that assumption.

The position of the atheist, then, is the only honest position. The atheist admits that he does not know how the turtle's shell originated, but he does not go on to contradict himself by claiming that he nevertheless knows that God originated it. However, as was pointed out earlier (see section I), the atheist may claim to know that God does not exist because no good reason has been given to support the belief that He does. Certainly, as we have seen, ignorance is not a good reason to believe that God exists.

The argument from ignorance of natural causes rests on a false assumption. This assumption is that our *knowledge* of nature corresponds exactly to nature as it is. Thus *ignorance* of natural causes would be the exact equivalent of the *nonexistence* of natural causes. But if this assumption were true, we would know everything there is to know. Since we plainly do not, the assumption is false and the argument based on it must be unsound.

We should note here that if science were to start accepting merely adequate explanations of puzzling phenomena, God would only be one possibility out of a crowd of such possible explanations. How could we decide among them? It would have been, for example, quite adequate to explain the common cold as the result of small invisible fairies entering people's noses and tickling tender nostrils with their tiny fingers. Primitive man was a specialist at imagining such explanations. He believed thunder to be the voice of angry cloud-spirits tossing spears of lightning at each other and crying tears of rain when wounded. The use of these merely adequate explanations is mythology, not science.

Today, of course, we are a bit more sophisticated than our primitive ancestors. Angry, spear-throwing warriors are no longer respectable; scientists now have the cultural prestige that tribal warriors once had. Instead of explaining things in the mythological terms of spear-throwing spirits, theists tend to employ a more modern mythology composed of scientific spirits. Theists claim that the turtle got its shell because a great scientific spirit named God engineered the design. Or that the universe started to expand because a great engineering spirit set a spiritual charge of spiritual dynamite and spiritually blew it up. And so on. Those theists who recognize the absurdity of their mythology try to give it respectability by redefining God as a "spiritual force" or (vaguely) something else—anything just as long as it is not so obviously a magnified version of man. But it should be noted that God is an adequate explanation only insofar as He resembles human beings, at least in the respect of having a mind. The theist is constantly insisting that mindless causes cannot explain the universe. He cannot have it both ways. His allegedly adequate explanation must be recognizable or run the risk of being totally inadequate after all.

The theist would do well to avoid the subject of science altogether. The evidence science does provide actually contradicts traditional theism. For instance, the Christian God is supposedly a wise planner, one who is not needlessly cruel. Now we know that plant-eating animals would soon exceed the limits of their food supply if their reproduction rate is not checked. Carnivores eat these animals thereby reducing the population to keep it within the limits of the food supply. Thus the balance of nature is maintained, and if God's planning is to be found anywhere it is to be found here. When a man interferes with the balance of nature by killing off carnivores, for example, the herbivores, which were formerly their prey, reproduce past the limits of their available food supply. Widespread starvation is the result.

Now if it is reasonable to see God's planning in the above example of the balance of nature, it is also reasonable to see God's planning in what follows. Bacteria and viruses which kill human infants, if unchecked, would keep infant mortality high thus diminishing effective reproduction so that the human population would fail to exceed its food supply. When human interference – in the form of medical advances – reduces infant mortality, and these advances are not accompanied by birth control or more efficient food production, overpopulation and widespread starvation result. The theist sees the plan of God in this natural balance, and points out that disasters may result from man's interference. The theist must, therefore, see the plan of God in the array of horrible diseases primarily responsible for infant mortality. The painful death of children must have been *deliberately planned* by God. Add to this the fact that a naturally adjusted birthrate – a form of God-designed birth control – could have achieved a balance of nature with more efficiency and less brutality, and we see what kind of planner God really is.

III. God and the Laws of Nature

The term "laws of nature" has led to much theistic speculation and argument. One popular position maintains that the term "law" implies the existence of a lawgiver. Such a view is clearly related to how people perceive the origin of social rules such as legislation, family regulations, customs, and so forth. If prescriptive laws impose orderly behavior on people, then the orderly behavior of nature must be the result of a similar body of laws. The heart of this argument, as with many theistic arguments, is that certain features of nature resemble the deliberateness which often accompanies the activity of the human mind, therefore these features are the result of the activity of a mind greater than man's.

The law–lawgiver analogy will not hold, however. Human laws imply the existence of minds which tell other minds what to do, rather than directing unconscious matter. No legislature ever passed a law forbidding water to drown people. Nature would have to be conscious in order to obey any prescriptive laws enacted by minds, whether human or divine. Laws of nature are not prescriptive; they are descriptive. The difference can be clearly seen in the following example. If a man disobeys a prescriptive law, the police would attempt to apprehend him. If objects habitually "disobeyed" the laws of gravity, these laws would have to be revised to account for such unusual behavior.

Perhaps the argument can be reconstructed to mean that the human mind imposes orderly behavior on the world within its grasp. Orderly behavior throughout nature could therefore be the result of God's mind imposing a similar orderly behavior on a larger scale. But the starting point of this version of the argument is plainly false. The human mind does not create orderly behavior in the artifacts it makes. On the contrary, human beings *make use* of the orderly behavior already existing as a characteristic feature of the materials from which such objects are made. They discover just what the orderly behavior of nature is and then employ this behavior for their own purposes. If nature had not been orderly from the outset, no one could ever build anything that would work. Without the laws of mechanics, no clock would ever function. Without the laws of electricity, no light-bulb would ever glow. Without the laws of chemistry, no car would ever start. There is no evidence that minds originate the kind of orderly behavior we employ in our artifacts. Minds only redirect existing orderly behavior so that the latter conforms to specific purposes. There is no reason to conclude that the orderly behavior of nature is caused by a mind. The theist's argument is that mind is a *known* source of some fundamental orderly behavior of nature, therefore mind is probably the source of *all* such behavior. But if it cannot be established that mind is the known source of *any* such behavior, then the conclusion that mind is probably the source of *all*—or, indeed, any—orderly behavior will not follow. Mind *might* be the source, but this bare possibility is no justification for the belief that it is in fact the source. The fact that a state of affairs *possibly* exists does not imply that it *probably* exists. Any state of affairs is possible but current conditions make only certain states probable. Furthermore, without evidence that minds originate this fundamentally ordered behavior, we have no evidence that they are even capable of doing so. The evidence we do have indicates that orderly behavior must exist *before* minds can impose their purposes on nature. It is therefore incorrect to argue that orderliness results from a mind imposing its purposes on nature.[3]

Arguments from natural law usually depend upon our sense of wonder as to why these laws are what they are. Why *this* state of affairs rather than some other? The feeling is that any specific state of affairs must be the result of someone's will, otherwise there would be no ultimate reason why things are ordered in one way and not another. Suppose a man wills that his arm move, and it does move; we say that his will is effective—it gets results. Now if we use this example of a mind's act of will as a model for explaining the existence of the present state of affairs, we will be no closer to an ultimate explanation. If God wills that a certain state of affairs should be realized and, as a matter of fact, it is realized, then his will is effective. However, there is one thing that cannot be the result of God's will: the fact that his will is effective. For if God's will is not effective, then nothing he wills would come about. It would follow that he could *not* will that his will become effective and, as a result, have it become effective. Unless God's will is *already* effective, he could not will it to become effective and have it in fact become effective. If God's will is *not* effective, God could not *make* it effective. Thus, if God's will *is* effective, God did not make it effective. So there is at least one state of affairs that *cannot* be dependent on God's will: namely, that his will is effective. If there is one state of affairs independent of God's will, then it cannot be true that *every* state of affairs must be dependent on God's will. It is therefore not true that the state of affairs existing in the universe must be dependent on God's will. We have cited an example of a state of affairs that cannot be the result of God's will; and where there is one such state of affairs, there may well be others.[4]

The usual sorts of countermoves brought to bear upon this kind of refutation will not succeed. The theist might object by saying that God is actually self–caused. But that is what the present argument has just shown to be impossible. God is not the cause of his own effective will. It might be said that God's mind is not subject to causality. But there is no reason whatsoever to accept a mind not subject to causality as a cause of any state of affairs. We accept mind as a possible explanation of particular states of affairs only because we are familiar with mind as the sort of entity which assists in bringing them about. If we are not merely to assume that God exists, we must concede that we are completely unfamiliar with minds which are not subject to causality.

If our familiarity with mind is the basis for accepting it as an explanation, then our lack of familiarity with un-caused mind should be grounds for not accepting that kind of mind as the foundation for explanations. If the basis for accepting an explanation is familiarity, then there is no basis for acceptance if there is no familiarity. This general point can be made clearer with an example. We are familiar with *human* beings as murderers, but we are not familiar with *Martian* beings as murderers. Therefore, if a murder is committed, it must be explained in terms of the actions of human beings, not Martians. Similarly, if we are to explain existing states of affairs in terms of minds, we must explain them in terms of minds with which we are familiar. This same point will apply to any attempt by the theist to characterize God as a necesary being or as self-explanatory. The theist must provide reasons to support such a claim. If the theist claims that the effectiveness of the will in familiar minds is self-explanatory, then there is no reason not to assume that the fundamental state of affairs obtaining in the universe is also self-explanatory. In both cases we would be referring to states of affairs other than those applying to God. If mental regularities are ultimate, then there is no reason why material regularities may not also be ultimate. It should be emphasized here that we are discussing the *effectiveness* of the will, not its supposed *freedom*.

One may wonder at the oddity of an argument from orderliness. The theist innocently demands a cause for orderliness, forgetting, of course, that "cause" presupposes "orderliness." Without the laws of causality, no causes would be operative. The laws of causality must therefore exist *before* any cause can operate. Therefore the laws of causality cannot be the *result* of any cause. These are laws which cannot be caused even by God.

A version of the argument from natural laws can be offered which rests upon estimates of probability. The argument claims that it is very improbable for the universe to have become law-governed by chance, since chaos is much more likely. Now there are an infinite number of different sets of possible natural laws. To give just one example: it is a natural law that gravity accelerates falling bodies in a vacuum at thirty-two feet per second per second. This acceleration could possibly have been thirty-three feet per second per second, or thirty-four . . . and so on to infinity. Thus, there are an infinite number of different sets of possible natural laws, and an infinite number of possible different law-governed universes. Therefore even if there are an infinite number of possible chaotic universes – universes not governed by natural laws – the probability would be fifty-fifty that a law-governed universe would exist. There would be as many potential instances of law-governed universes as there are non-law-governed universes. When one flips a coin, there are as many possible instances of heads as there are of tails and this is the basis for our judgment that the chance of getting tails is fifty-fifty. The same point holds for the chance of "getting" a law-governed universe. But we can go even further. A chaotic universe would by definition have no natural laws. Therefore no method exists to distinguish one possible chaotic universe from another in terms of natural laws. Since natural law is the only factor relevant in distinguishing one possible universe from another in this argument, we would be able to distinguish only a vague possible chaotic universe. Since we can distinguish an infinite number of possible law-governed universes, the probability is infinitely high that our universe could have been law-governed by chance.[5]

It has been argued that there are only two ways of explaining events: through the use of scientific explanation or in terms of choices made by minds. Scientific explanations of the orderly behavior of nature contain references to a more general observation of specific fundamental behavior. (The phenomenon of lightning, for example, can be explained as a special case of the behavior of electrons.) Therefore, when we reach the most pervasive and fundamental behavior of nature it can no longer be given a scientific explanation. Now there is only one other type of explanation, and if the most fundamental orderly behavior is to be explained at all, it must be explained by this type of explanation—that is, by choices made by minds. If we are not to consider fundamental order as unexplained brute fact, then we must describe it as a result of choice. If we do, all explanation of orderly behavior will ultimately be in terms of choice, which will simplify our understanding of the universe. This is a distinct advantage because science prefers the explanation which assumes the least.[6]

The point of this argument is that science has left the orderliness of nature as an unexplained brute fact. But a similar point applies to the orderliness of minds. Remember, the argument depends upon our knowledge of minds as the basis for explanation; the only minds we know are our own—and they certainly operate in an orderly manner. Our thoughts do not occur as a disorderly chaos. If we can simplify our explanation of order by claiming that it is ultimately understood in terms of the choices of minds, then we can also simplify it by claiming that it is equally explainable in terms of the order of nature. For the orderliness of minds could just as easily have been derivative from the order of nature as the other way around.

There is a clear application of this point to the question of God.[7] If we theorize that God's mind is the explanation of the orderly behavior of the universe, then what could be the explanation of the orderly behavior of God's mind? (Recall, again, that we are using as an explanation what we know to be true of minds, and we know they are orderly as well as—for the sake of argument—order-producing. Therefore the postulated mind of God must be orderly. Indeed, how could a disorderly chaos of a mind produce order in a universe?) There are only three possible explanations for the orderliness of God's mind. It could be just an unexplained brute fact. If so, we have merely substituted one brute fact for another, and have come no closer to the ultimate explanation of order. We must explain this new brute fact for the same reason that we had to explain the old brute fact. Moreover, it will not do to claim that mental orderliness is an ultimate fact. For we can make the same claim for material orderliness.

Another possibility is that the order of God's mind has been created by an even greater God. But then the greater God's mind would require an explanation in terms of a yet greater God . . . and so on endlessly. Now the point of offering explanations in terms of mind was to state the creative origin of order. But here order is just passed from a greater mind to a lesser mind with no creative origin. So there is no point at all in using this kind of mind-series as an explanation of orderliness. It would be just a complicated way of admitting that order has existed forever and that no mind dreamed it up out of nowhere in a creative act. And this is what the atheist asserts. Of course, if pressed, the theist could say that God's mind is self-explanatory, necessarily existing, or uncaused. But the problem with this response has already been brought out. We know of no such things as self-explanatory or necessarily-existing minds. The theist claims that mind should be the explanation of order because we know of minds which produce it. But we do not know of self-explanatory, necessarily-existing minds which produce it.

Therefore there is no justification for including them in the discussion. They are more mysterious than what they purport to explain and thus do not really serve as explanations. We increase our understanding by explaining things which are not well understood in terms of things which are better understood. In the case of necessarily existing minds we would be moving in the opposite direction.

In any case, the claim that God is a necessarily-existing being cannot save theistic arguments based on an orderly universe. Instead, such a claim will completely destroy them. If God exists necessarily, he cannot fail to exist. Therefore, he would exist whether the universe is orderly or chaotic. It follows that no argument based on the orderliness of the universe can resolve the question of God's existence.

Consider a parallel case. If I claim that John is home only when his car is in the garage, then I base my belief that he is home on the presence of his car. But if I claim that John is home whether or not his car is in the garage, I do not base my belief that he is home on the presence of his car. Similarly, if the theist claims that God exists necessarily—that He must exist regardless of the presence or absence of order in the universe—then the theist is no longer basing his belief in God on the presence of order in the universe. Instead he is offering a different argument, one that will be refuted later. (See the section "God and Existence.")[8]

It is sometimes argued that the possible sets of natural laws that permit life are only a few out of an infinite number of potential sets of laws. Therefore, the odds against natural laws permitting life are infinitely high. But we do have such natural laws. Therefore, they must have been planned. As a response, I ask you to consider a parallel case. There is a lottery in which a billion people are entered and you have only one ticket. The odds are one in a billion that you will win, and yet you win. Would we argue that the lottery result must have been planned because you won? No, because if it were reasonable to do so, then no matter who might have won we could also claim that the result was rigged. Reasoning which concludes that a lottery is rigged no matter who wins is plainly unsound. The odds may be infinitely high against our particular fortuitous set of natural laws, but the fact that we won the natural law lottery is no indication that it was rigged by God.

IV. God and Design

In one of its many versions, the design argument states that objects such as watches can be considered designed because we observe that they have an accurate adjustment of parts which produces a useful effect. The human eye also has an accurate adjustment of parts constructed so as to produce a useful effect. Therefore, if the watch was judged to be designed because it had an accurate adjustment of parts which produced a useful effect, then the human eye must be similarly judged.

This argument arrives at its conclusion—that the eye is designed—by starting with a claim about the way we identify watches as designed objects. It argues that we must identify products of God's design by the same method we use to identify watches as designed. The only examples the theist can use are instances—such as watches—which are not thought to be designed by God. The theist's argument *must* begin this way because any non-hypothetical argument must proceed from what is presumed to be true. Arguments supporting Divine design will be based upon examples where design is presumed. Without assuming God's existence, the only things presumed to be designed are objects not designed by God. Hence, to start with presumed examples of God's design would be to assume just what we are attempting to prove—namely, that there *are* such examples. Therefore, the only reliable method available for detecting design is the one we have successfully used to detect products not designed by God.

As was demonstrated in the preceding paragraph, the design argument must use the very same method to identify products presumably designed by God which has proven reliable in identifying products designed by beings other than God. The question, then, is this: How do we identify products which are designed by beings other than God? Are we to assume, as the design argument would have it, that this method consists of identifying an accurate adjustment of parts in the supposed product which together produce a useful effect?

In order to test whether this method is correct, let us imagine that we have landed on another planet. Assume that there really are intelligent non-human inhabitants on this planet but we do not see them. Having imagined these things, could we learn that the inhabitants exist just by examining the objects around us? Well, suppose the inhabitants constructed objects that resemble watches and guns. On seeing these things, we would immediately conclude that they were designed by intelligent beings. But suppose these beings constructed only living things that resembled cats and trees. We would never suspect that the planet was inhabited by intelligent beings if objects such as these were observed.[9]

What is the difference between cats and trees on the one hand, and watches and guns on the other? *All* of them have accurate adjustments of parts which produce some useful effect, so this cannot be the basis for identifying particular objects as designed. The real difference is this: things like watches and guns do not resemble the kind of objects found in nature. We do not find objects with steel springs and cogs existing naturally as in the case of cats and trees. Although trees are found growing throughout nature, we do not find them just popping up in the shape of wooden houses. Both trees and houses have an accurate adjustment of parts to produce useful effects, yet if we found a house on a new planet, we would regard it as evidence that the planet has intelligent inhabitants. We would not accept the presence of a tree as evidence that intelligent life exists.

What can be learned from the preceding example? The criterion for identifying products as designed by beings other than God is not that of an accurate adjustment of parts to produce a useful effect. Instead, it must be whether or not the supposed product *differs* from things (such as cats, trees or body organs) found in nature. And, of course, the design argument must employ only the criterion we ordinarily and successfully use to identify products designed by beings other than God. This is the only known indisputable criterion of design. The only possible conclusion, given what we know about the design argument, is that objects such as eyes are *not* designed by God.[10]

Now the preceding argument has established the method we must use to detect design. But it is still worthwhile to explore why no other alternative methods are possible.

Theists are impressed, for example, by the fact that the

eye is composed of many atoms which work together closely interacting to make possible a particular result—in this case sight. Theists claim that close, complex interaction of countless parts proves that the result produced is actually intended. This assertion is unfounded and an example should suffice as evidence to support my claim. Consider a random whirl of dust particles. All the particles composing it must interact to produce the exact distribution of particles which occurs. If only a single particle has moved contrary to its course, the exact arrangement of particles would have been different. We would never have recognized the change because all dust particles look alike to us, but the result would nevertheless have been different. Now, according to the theist's reasoning, the existence of this complex interaction of countless particles producing a specific result must indicate the presence of some intention. However, the result of a completely random, totally unplanned whirl of dust particles is exactly what we mean by an unintentional result. Clearly, reasoning which makes a demonstrably unintended result appear to be intended is fundamentally unsound.[11] Theists will, of course, want to say that in the case of the eye we are discussing "cooperation" of parts, and not merely their *interaction*. But cooperation is simply interaction to achieve an *intended* result. Therefore, if the theist refers to the interaction of parts as "cooperation," he is assuming the very point he is attempting to prove—namely, that a result was intended. Parts interact whether the result of their interaction is intended or not. Thus, if we are not to presume the truth or falsity of intention for the design argument, we must use a neutral term such as "interaction."

Consider another example of fantastically complicated causes interacting to produce an unintended result. I meet a total stranger from another city while on a bus trip. No one would describe such an insignificant meeting as planned. But notice the incredible number of causes which had to interact to produce this meeting. If our parents had not moved to their particular cities, if either he or I had been sick and thus unable to go on the bus trip, or if one or both of us had not had the money for busfare or the motive for the trip, etc. etc. – even to the causes of these causes stretching back to the beginning of the world – then we would not have met on that bus trip. The complex and exact interaction of causes to produce such a coincidental meeting is beyond all calculation, yet that would be no reason to consider it planned.

Any result – planned or unplanned – is what it is only because of the causes which interact to produce it. The proof of this is the fact that if the result is altered, then we know that the causes of it must have been altered as well. A gun's parts may be so constructed that it shoots straight. Another gun's parts may be so faulty that it explodes in the user's hand. There is no more or less interaction of parts producing the actual result in the one case than in the other. Yet the result in the first case is intended and the result in the second is not. We cannot tell that a group of parts interacting to produce a certain result have been put together intentionally to produce it merely because the parts work together. The obvious fact is that parts of anything always interact to produce the result they do produce, whether that result is intended or not. The reasoning of the theist is like that of the minister who saw God's design in observing that everybody – whether tall or short – had legs precisely long enough to reach the ground.[12]

Perhaps the theist could say that the interaction of parts to produce the proper result – not just *any* result – is the real indication of whether the result was intended. But what do we mean by the proper result? If we mean the *intended* result, then we would be saying that the cooperation of parts to produce an intended result proves that the result was intended. This would be true, of course; but whether or not the result was intended is precisely the question.

Perhaps the theist could say that interaction of parts to produce a *useful* result proves that the result was intended. But an object's capacity to be used for some purpose does not necessarily indicate that it was intended for some purpose. Stairs are designed for climbing, but they can be used for sitting. Tree branches just grow without apparent purpose but they can be used as clubs or walking sticks. The bodies of human beings are in fact used as food and breeding places for bacteria and viruses but this certainly does not imply that such is the purpose of human bodies. Even a random whirlwind of dust particles could be useful if there were beings who live only by absorbing energy from such things. Assuming they were intelligent beings, they might even decide that whirlwinds of dust were intentionally produced for their benefit. Whether any collection of parts ultimately proves useful depends on the user; it is not a characteristic of the object used. Stairs, branches, human bodies, and whirlwinds are all complex compositions of many atoms interacting to produce a particular result. It seems that the conjunction of complex interaction and usefulness is still not enough to indicate that the result produced is intended.

In his effort to establish a connection between some result and a particular intention the theist could say that the most economical interaction of parts producing a useful result would indicate that such a result is the purpose an alleged designer had in mind. Human bodies, for instance, must have been designed as something more than food for bacteria because there are too many parts which are not strictly needed for that purpose. But the test of economy cannot be used to establish the presence of a purpose. We do not know the alleged designer's intentions before applying the test of economy, for that is what we hope to discover by applying the test. How, then, can we know that this test will reveal his intentions? We can know this only by first knowing that the things he makes have no parts which are not necessary to bring about their intended use. But we cannot know such a fact without first knowing their intended use. And this is precisely what we do not know and why we are applying the test of economy. The theist could always *assume* that no unnecessary parts exist, but such an assumption implies the presence of intentions — a move that would ultimately prove useless. Perhaps we could get around this dilemma if God told us he produced only economical artifacts or if we knew of other examples of his handiwork which were economical. But if either of these conditions were fulfilled, then we would already know God exists and would have no further need for the design argument. An assumed designer might not be economical. He might produce extra parts as decoration for esthetic reasons.[13]

Thus far the theist has been arguing merely from his consideration of physical results and attempting to discover intentions behind them. Perhaps we should begin to suspect that he is moving in the wrong direction. Our discussion might prove more fruitful if we start with intentions and compare them with the physical results to which they lead.

Let's suppose that we had never before seen a watch. How would we know its purpose from simply looking at it? Might it not be intended as a toy to teach children how to count from one to twelve and to amuse them with its ticking?

Obviously we can know its purpose only by first knowing the intention in the mind of its designer. Purpose is not physical in nature although it can be expressed in physical form. Purpose is a mental fact. It can be detected only by comparing the designer's intentions with the actual physical result. The proof of this is that we consider a designed thing as designed only to the extent that we know it expresses the intention of its designer. For example, suppose I intend to build an ordinary house, but the result of my efforts is a house with a sagging roof, uneven windows, and leaning walls. If you knew the defects were unintentional, you would know they were not part of the design of the house. It is possible, however, that I deliberately built this wreck of a house to be exactly the way it is—perhaps as part of a movie set. In that case, all of the result would be intentional; all of the house would be designed. How could one tell that this was actually the case? Clearly, only by knowing my intentions.

Now if purpose can be detected only by comparing the designer's intentions with the physical result, then before we can detect God's purpose, we must first know his intentions. And before we can know his intentions we must first know he exists—for he cannot have intentions unless he does exist. Therefore the argument from design cannot prove God's existence because we must first know he exists before we can know anything is designed by him.[14]

The above reasoning is generally obscured by the fact that we could detect unseen intelligent inhabitants of another planet just by examining their designed products—a point I raised earlier in this handbook. But we could detect them only when the products they design differ from things (such as eyes) found in nature. This is because we know that our designing intentions are usually expressed in such physical forms as watches, but not in natural things such as eyes. We can identify a thing as designed, even when we do not know its purpose, only if it resembles the things we make to express our purposes.

The words "resembles the things which express our purposes" should be given some content. What specifically is this resemblance? The principal relevant resemblance is in the materials which compose designed objects. We *know* that certain kinds of matter such as iron and stone are stubbornly unchanging unless they are melted or molded or hammered and chiselled into some useful shape by intelligent beings. We *know* that, without intervention by intelligent beings, these substances just lie on the ground rusting or eroding, as they have for millions of years. However, unless the theist assumes what he is trying to prove, he cannot claim that we know that the compounds which compose *living* matter could not have gradually developed over millions of years into living organisms without intervention by an intelligent being. This claim is precisely the *conclusion* of his argument and thus cannot be employed to reach that conclusion. We *can* argue from the fact that steel watches are designed to the conclusion that any unfamiliar, complex, and useful object composed of steel is designed. We can argue in this way because we know that iron, which is not intentionally altered by intelligent beings, undergoes no significant changes except rusting. But we cannot argue from the fact that steel watches are designed to the conclusion that eyes are designed. The relevant point of such a comparison would be the *known* inertness of the materials involved. And we must admit that only the material composing the watch is *known* to be inert, otherwise we commit the fallacy of assuming what we are trying to prove. After all, we can argue from the fact that stone statues are sculpted to the conclusion that stone buildings are constructed. But we cannot argue from the fact that stone statues are sculpted to the conclusion that — for example — snowflakes are carved. Water vapor is not as inert as stone. Freeze stone and it remains unchanged. Freeze water vapor and it forms into snowflakes. It is worthwhile to add here that one of the favorite examples of theists, that of a whirlwind of dust particles randomly forming a man's body, commits the same fallacy as the comparison of watches and eyes. Just as the parts of eyes are not molded out of steel, human bodies are not composed of dust particles. Human bodies are composed of matter with very different characteristics from those of steel and dust. Watches and dust, therefore, are simply irrelevant to the issue.

The design argument is an argument from the similarity of man-made and natural objects. Among man-made objects, all the apparent design is intentional. This leads to the theist's rule that examples of apparent design are examples of intentional design. The design argument then proceeds as follows. In the case of man-made objects, we know first that they have apparent design, second that examples of apparent design are examples of intentional design, and third that man-made objects are designed by minds. In the case of natural objects we know first that they have apparent design and second that examples of apparent design are also examples of intentional design. Therefore, we can conclude that the third characteristic of man-made objects also obtains in the case of natural objects: that natural objects are designed by minds.

But the rule which says that examples of apparent design are examples of intentional design cannot be substantiated in the realm of natural objects without assuming the very thing that is to be proved. For it is precisely the assertion that all examples of apparent design are examples of intentional design which is being questioned by the atheist. To assume that intentional design is or is not true with respect to natural objects would be to presume the truth or falsity of the conclusion for the design argument. But if the truth of the rule remains an open question for natural objects, this destroys the close similarity of natural objects and man–made objects. The only similarity left is that of apparent design. This similarity cannot establish that natural objects are made by minds precisely because such a conclusion requires first that all examples of apparent design are shown to be examples of intentional design. And this is exactly what must be left an open question. Now if we wish to retain the close similarity of man–made and natural objects, we can leave the question of intentional design open for both of them. But this move utterly destroys the argument since the latter is based on the truth of the rule that examples of apparent design are examples of intentional design.[15]

An interesting variation of the design argument asks us to consider a group of small rocks arranged to spell out the sentence "George Washington was the first president of the United States." If we believe this arrangement to be accidental, then we must believe that no information was intended to be conveyed by the arrangement. Consequently, we cannot conclude on the basis of this sentence alone that George Washington was the first president. (Other sentences written in history books may convince us of this, but we know they were not accidental.) Note the parallel case of our eyes which convey information to us. If the structure of our eyes is accidental (that is, not intended), then the information they provide is no more reliable than the information that the accidentally–produced sentence gave us. Therefore, if we rely on our eyes to give us correct information, we must believe they are the result of intentional design.[16]

The weakness of this argument lies in the fact that a sentence conveys information only because the users of a particular language intentionally agree that it does. Languages — and therefore sentences — are the purposeful products of agreements about the meanings of sounds and marks. This is demonstrated by the fact that someone who does not speak some particular language can look at a sentence written in that language and get no meaning from it, no matter how clearly he may see it. The fact that a language conveys information only because intelligent beings agree about its meaning indicates that the idea of purpose must be involved in all examples of sentences. But purpose need not be involved in examples of eyes conveying information. Seeing a fire is not an indication that there is a fire merely because there is agreement among intelligent beings that that is what seeing a fire indicates. The comparison between written sentences and eyes is therefore faulty.[17]

In general, the design argument relies on the assumption that everything which serves a useful purpose must be designed by a mind. But this assumption contains the requirement that minds must be designed for the purpose of designing. For if minds were not constructed in such a way that they are able to make plans, they could not develop, create, and design useful things. Therefore, if all mental processes must be the result of the way minds are constituted, then it must be untrue that all things which serve a useful purpose have been designed by minds. Otherwise, God's mind (or any mind) would have had to have been designed before it could possess its own capacity for planning. If purposeful design must precede and make possible all mental processes, then clearly not all design for a purpose can be derived from these mental processes. Since there can be purposeful design which is not mind dependent, then the human eye may well be a good example. After all, we do not see God designing eyes the way we can see men designing watches; both God and watches work toward an end.[18]

Having summarized the whole argument against the notion of universal design by an omnipotent Deity, I will now provide additional support for its various parts. First, it was stated above that minds must have been designed for the purpose of designing useful things much the same as watches are designed for showing the time. Now the nature of the human mind is such that it is motivated by the desire for food, sex, and by the fear of death. This would indicate that human minds are designed to promote human survival. Both watches and human minds have elements that work together toward a specific end. Like the eye, the mind promotes human survival also. Human minds promote the survival of the specie by generating plans, by developing and designing the materials available to them. A mind considers some things as desirable and other things as undesirable before it can be motivated to plan. This is obviously true because plans are the means for attaining desired goals, or for avoiding particular situations. In order to be motivated to plan, God's mind must also find specific things desirable or undesirable. Consequently, there is as much evidence that God's mind is designed as that the human mind is designed. The evidence that God's mind is designed is just as strong as the evidence that a watch is designed.

To attack this argument the theist must demonstrate that there is one particular relevant difference between minds and material things—that only material objects are capable of being designed. But there are reasons why this attack cannot succeed. I shall address this issue by offering the atheist's claims against such a relevant difference and then discuss the theist's responses.

First, it makes sense to refer to minds as capable of being designed. A thing that can be designed is something that could have been different from the way it actually is—could have been shaped differently, or put together differently, or composed differently in some respect. Minds can differ in many details such as content and characteristics, although not in physical shape or material composition. There are in fact an unlimited number of ways in which they can differ. Thus the composition of a mind can be infinitely complex—at least as much as spatial combinations of matter. Minds can differ in personality, desires, and skills. Most importantly, minds can differ widely in specific knowledge; that is, the bits of information stored by the mind could be in many different combinations. And where there is difference, it can be the result of deliberate planning. People can be and are deliberately taught, trained or brainwashed to think, believe, and act the way they do. Parents to a large extent, shape and mold the minds of their children. Most of us believe that children should be "brought up" properly, thereby recognizing the designer's responsibility for what is designed.

Second, that which is designed can function properly or improperly. Some watches keep the exact time while others run too fast. Certain guns hit the mark while others may veer to the left or right. Clearly, minds differ in their ability to function. There are both idiots and geniuses. A baby's mind is incapable of planning until it is altered by its environment; that is, until it is taught. In order to be capable of planning an eye, God's mind must obviously have more knowledge and ability than that of a baby or an idiot. Just as the eye is perfectly designed for the function of seeing, God's mind is perfectly designed for the function of planning such things as eyes.

Unless all of its parts are put together in a certain way a watch will not work properly to indicate the time. So too, without relevant bits of information and the skill to put them together a mind will be unable to design. It is true that minds can work on their own to obtain skills and knowledge but even this requires much pre-existing skill and information. Information and the conditions underlying the developing of skill must come from an environment external to the mind and this fact simply pushes the question of the origin of design back only to be addressed at some later time. The mind, in acquiring skills and knowledge, begins to recognize and learn from the preexisting forms of design within its environment. This is evident today when even the most original inventor produces new variations on the inventions of others. Even the first human beings had many instances of pre-existing design to teach them what to do. For example, the wheel was just a modification of a rolling stone or log. A club was an extension of the human arm. An axe assumed the role of an artificial tooth. (Note the parallel between a beaver gnawing wood and a lumberjack chopping it.)

To sum up, minds, much like eyes, are complex and possess useful functions. If all eyes must be the product of design, then so too must every mind. Ultimately, there must be a concept of design not dependent on the notion of mind. If so, eyes as well as minds may be examples of such non-purposeful design. I have argued that we have as much reason to believe that minds were designed as we have to believe that eyes were designed. Observation indicates that both have been subject to modification, yet minds were never invented. Therefore, eyes may never have been invented either.

The theist, in reviewing these arguments in support of the claim that minds are indeed designed, might object that God's mind is different from ordinary minds in that it had no beginning. But this would be to claim that God's mind has always been adjusted in such a way that it can design such things as eyes. But if the theist can make such a claim, then the atheist would be equally justified in claiming that matter has always been adjusted in such a way that it can form itself into such things as eyes. This would be no more odd than the fact that seeds are adjusted to grow into plants.

Theists might retort by claiming that stone cannot form itself into a statue and steel does not put itself together to form watches. Of course there are kinds of matter that cannot organize themselves, but, by the same token, there are minds that cannot plan. We do not want to argue that planning initiated by minds is impossible merely because babies and idiots are unable to plan. Therefore, we cannot argue that living matter is incapable of organizing itself simply because stone and steel cannot do so. Both matter and mind have their limitations.

Finally, it will not do to object that God's mind exists necessarily, while nothing else does. This move has been dealt with already in the section on "God and the Laws of Nature."

The strength of the design argument lies in the observation that human minds design and build various artifacts. Thus, there is no question that the argument attempts to establish the existence of a great mind. This mind, in order to plan and build a universe, must be very knowledgeable. As we have seen, minds must have specific characteristics suitable for the functions they are to perform; and God is no exception to this rule.

Now is it not absurd to believe that a magnified version of a well-educated man's mind has existed either forever or timelessly? Certainly it is no less absurd than believing that a dog's mind trained to fetch, roll over, and play dead has existed either forever or timelessly. It seems unlikely that minds—canine, human or godly—with any kind of effective training for their functions could have been existing from eternity. The idea of a mind seems to include the idea of an environment which has shaped it, and this would require that the mind came into being. Theists have emphasized those features of the human mind which serve their purpose while neglecting to take into account other features which do not conform to their goal.

A variation of the design argument is the assertion that complex objects are not the result of chance events. For example, the eye could not have resulted from a mere chance combination of atoms; therefore, it must have been planned.

The theist's concept of chance must be investigated to determine why he does not consider it likely that chance produced an eye. He usually explains it by saying that, when blind chance operates, there are billions of different possible combinations of atoms that could come into being. Since chance is blind and no more likely to result in one combination than another, all possible combinations have an equal probability of occurring. The combination which would compose an eye is only one out of many billions of possible combinations; the odds against its occurrence are billions to one. According to the theist, if this one out of all those billions *does* occur, then it must have been the result of a deliberate choice.

The problem here, of course, is this: if the combination of atoms composing the eye is only one out of billions of possible combinations, then so is every other possible combination. Take whatever combination you wish; there are always billions of others that could have happened. Thus, if the chances are billions to one against the eye combination, then the same probability would hold for any other combination. And yet, even in a random shuffling of atoms, one combination would occur despite the chances against it. When it did occur it would be just as improbable as the eye. Would we consider a completely disorganized clump of atoms the result of some plan just because its existence was as improbable as the eye? Then why consider the existence of the eye as a planned event just because it is improbable?[19]

To clarify this point, consider a game of poker. If one player were to be dealt four aces, he would consider this result less likely than being dealt any other series of cards. Yet the odds against *any* four particular cards being dealt are exactly the same. Each card is only one out of fifty-two, each card being one of a kind in the deck. There is no way that one specific combination could be more likely than some other. The numbers marked on the cards have no mystical influence over what cards are eventually dealt. If the numbers were all magically changed around during a deal, the same physical cards would be dealt, though their numbers would be different. Or if the rules of the game were changed so that four aces had no special value, while a "random" series such as the two of hearts-four of clubs-seven of spades-king of clubs beat all other combinations, then this last set of cards would now appear less likely than any other. The fact is that we mistakenly tend to consider a meaningful combination of anything—cards or atoms—as necessarily less likely than an insignificant combination.

To see this point still more clearly, let's consider an example of a completely unplanned, chance result—a game of dice. When tossed, two dice will turn up in one out of thirty-six possible combinations. All combinations have an equal likelihood of turning up. That is why tossing dice is considered a game: each person has an equal chance that his combination will turn up. The significance of the game centers upon its unplanned result. If the result had been planned, then the identity of the winner would have been known before the game began. But the identity of the winner must be left to blind chance. The dice, we say, should not be loaded.

The same principle would apply to any result of a chance process. If there are only two possible explanations the working out of a plan or blind chance—then in an unplanned process each particular possible alternative result would have the same probability of occurring. Chance is blind and does not favor one possible combination over another, but planning does. With chance as the operative feature, all possible combinations are equally likely; with planning operative, one result becomes more likely than any of the others.

Now the atoms which compose the eye could have combined into billions of other different, possible combinations. Yet if the results of the combining of atoms were unplanned, every particular possible combination would have had an equal chance to occur. Therefore, if any of the possible combinations had happened instead of the eye, this particular combination would have been equally as unlikely—just as improbable—as the eye. If this clump of atoms is as improbable as the eye, and if we have no reason to call such a clump designed, then we have no reason to call the eye designed merely because it has a low probability. To assert otherwise is contradictory. It is to say that equal probabilities are not in fact equal.

At this point, a theist might claim that no one would consider the Bible to be the chance result of print falling together. The suggestion would then be made that there must be something wrong with the above reasoning. And of course there is, but this fact does not help the theist. We have been using the only concept of chance that the theist could have used to prove his point and we have shown that it does not in fact demonstrate his claim. Now the theist himself brings up an objection which inadvertently shows that his concept of chance is inadequate. In calculating chances we do not simply take note of how many alternative outcomes are possible and then claim they are all equally possible. We do this in the case of dice only because dice are deliberately designed so that all outcomes are equally possible. In the real world, few things work out so neatly. Instead, we take note of how often one particular result takes place and how often another happens; the ratio between them is the chance that the one will occur rather than the other. When we drop a rock we see that it always falls. We do not assume that all possible directions the rock could take are equally likely such that the chances are one out of all possible directions that the rock will fall *downward*. There is in fact no chance at all that it will fall anywhere but straight down. However, if on half of the occasions when we released a rock we saw it fall up and half the time we saw it fall down, then we could say that the chances of the rock falling down were fifty-fifty.

Now in the case of print scattered at random, we have never seen it produce the Bible, although we may have seen it scattered many times. Whenever print does produce the Bible, it has done so deliberately. So we can say there is no chance at all that print scattered at random will produce the Bible, and that if we see print spelling out the Bible, the chances are overwhelming that it was the result of planning.

But what about the human eye? The origin of the eye is the end product of some process — be it design or chance — but we have never witnessed that process. We have not seen eyes evolve, nor have we seen God make them. So how can we state any estimate of the chances for eyes coming to exist without planning? We have no evidence upon which to base our probabilities. Clearly, if we had never seen anything fall either up or down, we would never be able to calculate the chances of a thing falling down.[20]

The theist assumes a concept of chance in which every alternative result is equally possible. Unfortunately, this kind of chance can compete successfully with design. If the theist then abandons this concept of chance and uses a more realistic approach, he has no basis at all to make judgments about the likelihood of eyes originating by chance.

Theists may invoke the second law of thermodynamics as a last attempt at shoring up the chance-argument. This law implies that the universe tends, in the long run, toward states of lesser organization. This may be generally true, but it is not locally and temporarily true and is therefore irrelevant to local and temporary phenomena such as eyes. After all, oil mixed with water tends to separate into a layer of water topped by a layer of oil; the tendency here is toward a more organized result. Gaseous nebulae tend to contract to form stars, a result more organized than diffused gases. Mixed atoms of hydrogen and oxygen tend to combine when heated to form molecules with an exact ratio of two hydrogen to one oxygen. Quick–frozen water vapor forms snowflakes with complex designs. The second law of thermodynamics therefore lends no support to theistic arguments based upon the concept of blind chance.[21]

The only sense of "chance" which the theist can use is "unplanned," for it must contrast with "planned." However, if the theist's argument is that the eye, for example, could not have been created by an unplanned process, then he has denied the theistic explanation. Consider how a mind creates a plan. Insofar as the plan is created — to the extent that it is truly original — it cannot be the result of a plan. If I have previously planned the specific plan I will devise in the future, then *I will by that very fact have already made that plan*. The act of planning the plan would itself *be* the creation of that plan. Any plan which would precede and guide the creation of a plan would already *be* the plan we are creating and could itself have no plan to precede and guide it. For if there were such a preceding plan *it* would be the plan we are creating. Created plans must begin somewhere without being derived from preceding plans, or else the plans would not be created but rather eternal. It is therefore impossible to claim that the creation of a plan was itself the result of a plan. If the creation of a plan must itself be unplanned, then its creation must be the result of "chance" as the theist must use the term. The theist, then, cannot deny that in the final analysis the plan of the eye is the result of a "chance" process. With respect to both theories — theistic or atheistic — the eye must ultimately be the result of "chance." Therefore the theist cannot argue that the atheistic theory is false merely because it attributes the eye to "chance."

The theist might object that God has absolute fore-knowledge and therefore is not creative. This would be to claim that God's plans are eternal, never created. But in that case, God's production of an eye (for example) would be merely a mechanical exercise in copying stored information, in the same way a carrot seed draws on its genetic information to develop a carrot. A God with absolute fore-knowledge can do nothing that mere matter cannot do. The theist is therefore faced with a dilemma. Either God is creative, in which case the theistic theory claims that the eye is the result of "chance," or God is not creative, in which case the eye would be the result of mechanical reproduction.

Finally, we should note that the design argument's proper conclusion is merely that natural objects are the product of intelligent construction. This implies nothing of a God or gods. Suppose that the universe was cooperatively constructed by several generations of billions of minor ghostly beings no one of whom was more intelligent or powerful than the average human being. These non-material individuals could not be gods, because—as individuals—they are not superior to human beings. Their power would come from their *combined* effort and knowledge. And all of them working together would be no more a god than the human race itself is a super-being. The design argument, even if successful, does not come close to implying the existence of a God or gods.

V. God and the Universe

The existence of the universe is often cited as a reason for believing in God. One popular argument contends that, since any object we encounter is assumed to have some explanation for its existence, we must — if we are consistent — assume that the universe also has an explanation. After all, the universe can be considered a very large collection of objects.

It is true that we assume the existence of an explanation for anything we encounter. But there is a necessary (if not sufficient) condition grounding this assumption: other objects must exist in addition to the thing in need of an explanation so that there will be a collection of possibilities through which we can search to find the explanation. Normally, when we are seeking to explain an object *in the universe* we know that we have the thing to be explained plus everything else that exists, wherein the explanation may be found. But if we are searching for an explanation *of the universe,* we do not know there is something other than the thing to be explained. That is precisely what the argument (and the theist) is trying to prove. Therefore the following difference can be noted between familiar, explainable things and the universe as a whole. The necessary condition of a demand for an explanation is satisfied in the case of familiar, explainable things regardless of whether God exists. But the necessary condition of a demand for an explanation is satisfied in the case of the *universe* only if the conclusion to the theist's argument is correct. Therefore, if we do not assume the very point the theist is trying to prove, we do not know that a demand for an explanation makes sense for the universe as a whole. We cannot simply assume the theist is correct. He must prove his point. The plausibility present when expecting an explanation for things *within* the universe does not necessarily exist when the universe itself is considered.[22]

Undoubtedly there are statements that can be made about objects *within* the physical universe which cannot be made about the *physical universe* itself. For example, an object can be above or below another object but the physical universe cannot be above or below another object. The physical universe comprises all the objects there are; there would be no other objects it could be above or below. Whether the relation of cause and effect has a clearer application to the universe than the relation of above and below is an open question. (Of course, if we found that our physical universe was just one of many physical "universes," then we would have discovered that our physical "universe" was just a part of a larger universe. But we use the term 'universe' to mean *all* the physical objects that exist *anywhere.*)

The argument, which contains an explanation of the

universe, attempts to conclude with an ultimate explanation of all that exists. Unless an ultimate explanation can be attained, there would be no point in going beyond various explanations within the universe. God would just be an extra unnecessary explanation that would eventually need an explanation of its own. This difficulty is summed up in the question: "If God made the universe, who made God?" Now in order to conclude that God is an ultimate explanation, the theist must consider God to be self-explanatory. But it is utterly impossible for God to be self-explanatory. Theists usually consider God's existence to be part of His essence and maintain that this renders God self-explanatory. But what do we mean by a certain characteristic being part of the essence of a thing? The essence of a thing is *what* it is. The essence of a table, for example, is whatever is common to all particular instances of tables. Having a flat surface on top is a characteristic which is part of the essence of being a table. But the fact that anything that is a table must have a flat surface does not explain why this particular thing was constructed as a table—that is, why it *is* a table. It merely explains why the thing must have a flat surface *if* it is a table. Similarly, the fact that God has an essence which includes existence would not explain why God is a being which has this particular essence. It only explains why he must exist *if* he has the particular essence he happens to have. Therefore God is certainly not self-explanatory since reference to his essence does not explain why he *has* that particular essence.[23]

The theist often maintains that parts of the universe are contingent, therefore the sum of all these parts must also be contingent and, in the end, dependent for its existence on a necessary being: God. The point of the argument is that a contingent fact cannot support itself; it must ultimately depend on a necessarily true fact. The relationship of dependence is an unfortunate example on which to base such an argument. Each member of the human race is dependent on other members for his social life. But it does not follow that the human race as a whole is dependent on non-human beings for *its* social life. The human race is dependent on nothing outside of itself for its social life. Therefore, it does not follow that just because every part of the universe is dependent we can conclude that the whole universe is dependent.

But what exactly does the theist mean by saying that the parts of the universe are contingent? The theist could mean that everything properly called contingent is dependent on something else for its existence. But if this is what he means, then we have no reason to believe that the fundamental parts of the universe (which combine to form contingent things) are themselves contingent. For all we know the ultimate sub-atomic particles which compose the universe just exist, being dependent on nothing. If the theist says they depend on God, then he is assuming what he has to prove. Remember, if the theist argues that God's existence is based upon the contingent nature of the various parts comprising the universe, he must first prove that these components are contingent. The theist often responds to such a challenge by pointing out that mere sub-atomic particles may be imagined not to exist, therefore they are in some sense contingent. But what needs to be established is the dependence of such particles on something else for their *actual* existence, not for their existence in the imagination.

The theist may mean by 'contingent' something other than merely dependent. When he claims that a thing is contingent, the theist often means that it is possible for the object to have been otherwise than it is. Let's accept this definition and construct an argument to see where it leads. The universe could have been otherwise than it is. In order to have a complete explanation of its characteristics, we must conclude that it results from a fact which could not have been otherwise. Now this fact must be the existence of a being who could not fail to have the characteristics he possesses. This being is God.

There are only two possibilities: either God chose to create the universe as it is and could have chosen otherwise, or else he had to create the universe as it is and could not have done otherwise. Both possibilities ruin the contingency argument.

Suppose God could have chosen otherwise and yet chose to create the universe as it is. Then the specific characteristics of the universe depend on a choice that might have been otherwise. The universe, therefore, despite the introduction of God as its explanation, still depends ultimately on a fact that might have been otherwise: namely, God's choice. (God's existence, by itself, does not explain the characteristics of a created thing; God must first choose to create it. Nor do God's characteristics explain his particular choice. For if they did, the choice could not have been otherwise—a possibility we will deal with below.) Now if the universe resulted from a fact that is as contingent as the universe (both the choice and the universe might have been otherwise), then we have explained the universe by means of a contingent fact and have therefore not given it a complete explanation. For the point of the theist's argument is this: a fact that *could* have been otherwise can be completely (or ultimately) explained only by a fact that could *not* have been otherwise (a necessary truth).

Since God's choice is not of this type, there is no proof of God here.[24]

But suppose we select the other possibility and claim that the universe depends for its characteristics on God's creative act and that this act could not have been otherwise. It follows that the universe could not have been otherwise. But the starting point of the argument was that the universe *could* have been otherwise. That is what the theist means by 'contingent.' On this horn of the dilemma, the theist's argument cannot even get started. Of course, the theist might point out that, on this second interpretation, the universe is dependent on God's necessarily existing act and therefore an argument to God's existence could be based on that dependence. But that argument would just commit the fallacy of assuming to be true what one is trying to prove. In effect it would be returning to the definition of contingency as dependence, and we have already refuted the argument based upon that interpretation.[25]

The attempt to base an argument for the existence of a necessary being on the existence of contingent objects and events is a misguided venture. A necessary being is defined as a being who exists necessarily. It follows that a necessary being would exist regardless of the existence of contingent beings. Whether or not there are contingent beings a necessary being would exist, since it could not fail to exist. It follows that no argument from the existence of contingent beings can have any thing to do with whether a necessary being exists. This point can be illustrated as follows. If it is claimed that John is home only when his house lights are on, then the fact that the lights are on will be the basis on which we decide that he is home. But if it is claimed that John is home regardless of whether his lights are on, then the fact that his lights are on is not the basis on which we decide that John is home. Similarly, if God would exist regardless of the existence of contingent beings, then one cannot base an argument for His existence on the existence of contingent beings.[26]

It is clear from the above demonstration that no argument from contingent (non-necessary) facts can establish that God (considered as a necessary being) exists. The only thing we have left upon which to base such an argument is the idea of a necessarily-existing being. How can we arrive at the actual existence of a thing merely by considering the idea of it? An idea can guarantee its truth only if the denial of it is self-contradictory. But it is not self-contradictory to say, "I have the idea of a being which cannot fail to exist, but there is no being which cannot fail to exist." This sentence makes perfectly good sense. It is merely a claim that all beings can fail to exist, although we have the idea of a being that cannot fail to exist. The sentence just means that the phrase "a being which cannot fail to exist" refers to nothing; it has no application at all.

It *would* be self-contradictory to say, "There is a being which cannot fail to exist, but there is no being which cannot fail to exist." But this would be to assume that the being exists, which is what the argument must prove. Merely saying that there is an idea of a being which cannot fail to exist is obviously not equivalent to saying that there actually *is* a being which cannot fail to exist.

Another argument for God's existence results from our observations of chain reactions. Theists sometimes argue that an object which is in motion must have attained that motion from another object which was previously in motion. This transfer of motion could not have proceeded forever without beginning; therefore God must have started it.

This argument contains several fallacies. First, even if it is granted that a thing cannot move itself, it does not follow that something else must have moved it. It could simply have always been in motion without ever having been moved. Why should rest be considered more natural than motion? After all, it is as difficult to stop something as it is to start it. We do not usually realize this because friction, gravity, and obstacles tend to halt movement on the earth. But anyone who has ever caught a tossed baseball will testify that it was quite difficult—even painful—to halt its motion. Objects tend to continue in their state of (relative) rest or motion, unless interfered with by other objects. (This is the physical law of inertia.)

It is true that theists generally intend the term 'motion' in this argument to apply to a process of reduction from potentiality to actuality. Once a process has been actualized, it is maintained; it cannot bring itself back to a state of potentiality and begin the process again. The relevant example here is a domino toppling over. If we consider the movement in the universe as comparable to the movement of one big domino, then it must have been set up to "fall down," so to speak. But there is no reason to compare the universe to a single domino. If potentiality and actuality are relevant here, we might consider all the processes in the universe as comparable to a row of dominoes toppling one after the other. Therefore since motion is as natural as rest there is no reason why we may not consider succeeding states of the universe to be like an endless row of dominoes toppling one after the other.

It may be true that intermediate events do not occur if they are not caused by *earlier* events, but it does not follow that they would fail to occur if not nudged by an absolutely first event. There seems to be no reason to deny that the series of events has no beginning, each event always being preceded by yet an earlier event. Compare a row of dominoes endlessly long (corresponding to successive phases of a finite universe) which has always been toppling a domino at a time. One could ask what began the dominoes' movement in the first place. But this is just to assume that there *was* a first place. And this is what the theist is attempting to prove. One could then say: "Take away the first domino falling and there would be no subsequent dominoes falling." Denying that there was a first domino is not the equivalent of taking away any particular domino. If I deny that the year 1 A.D. was the first year there ever was, I am not taking away the year 1 A.D. It was still there. I am just denying that it was the first year there ever was.[27]

The theist could object that the idea of a series of changes is not conceivable without the notion of a beginning. But it is at least as conceivable as a God who exists either without beginning or timelessly. One could object that an infinitely long series of events cannot be completed and the present time could not have been reached if past time were infinite. Yet if the series had no beginning, then there was no event which happened infinitely long ago — just as, in a series of events which has no end there is no last event which will occur some time in the future. Having no beginning obviously means that no matter how long ago an event happened, there are others which happened before it — just as having no end means that no matter how far in the future an event occurs, another will occur after it.[28] Besides, even if we suppose past time to have had a beginning, this would not mean God exists. For we assume that every event *within* time has a cause, yet this might not apply to the beginning of time itself because the commencement of time would not be an event *within* time. If time might have been nonexistent, then so might causality. The universe and time might have just popped into existence without a cause. This is just as conceivable as having a cause operate when there is no time in which it can operate. It certainly would appear that the existence of time is necessary to the functioning of causality. A cause precedes its effect in time. Therefore if time had a beginning, time itself could have no cause.

Finally, brief note must be taken of the fact that the universe is expanding—which points to its origin in a gigantic explosion. Did God set it off? There seems no reason to think so. The "explosion" could simply be a rebound from a gigantic collapse which had no beginning. After all, if we step into a room and see a ball flying into the air from the floor, we naturally assume it first fell to the floor and then bounced.

VI. God and Existence

In our consideration of various theist arguments we have occasionally encountered the suggestion that God is self-explanatory or necessarily-existing. This suggestion forms the basis of an argument for God's existence. In refuting it, we will also be refuting the basis for the theistic retreat to God's self-explanatory nature. This section is therefore supplementary to the three previous sections on "God and the Laws of Nature," "God and Design," and "God and the Universe."

The argument we will consider runs as follows. We have the idea of God, therefore God exists in our understanding. The idea of God is that of a being than which nothing greater can be conceived. But if God exists only in the understanding, it would be possible to conceive a being greater than God—that is, a being which exists not only in the understanding but also in actuality. But it is impossible for God to exist only in the understanding since by definition we cannot conceive anything greater than God. Therefore God exists in actuality.[29]

The argument depends on a distinction between existence in the understanding and existence in actuality: the latter is *greater* than the former. If there is a real difference in the two kinds of existence, then the argument cannot proceed by proving that existence in actuality is part of what we *understand* by the term 'God.' For if existence in actuality is different from existence in the understanding, then to say that existence in actuality is part of what we *understand* by the term 'God' is just to claim that God exists as an actual being *in the understanding*. This is quite different from proving that God exists as an actual being in some manner other than that of the understanding. It is merely to claim that nothing which does not actually exist can be understood to be God.[30]

VII. God and the Mind

Theists sometimes argue that matter cannot create mind, therefore God must exist to create it. It is pointed out that mind is quite different from matter. How, then, can we imagine that mere changes in matter could produce a mind? An effect cannot be "higher" or "greater" than its cause. A river cannot rise above its source; one cannot remove from a sack what was not first put into it. Therefore, mind could never have been created by that which is not a mind.

In reply we can point out that the capacity of matter to create mind has been denied merely because matter has no capacity to create matter. The examples commonly given — a stream and its source, a sack and its contents — are purely material. One cannot remove from a sack what was not first put into it because matter cannot create matter. The sack does not create its contents. But the point of the theist's argument is that mind is not matter. However, the argument has not produced any reason to deny that matter can create mind. It has shown only that matter cannot create matter. Any attempt to prove matter cannot create mind would have to depend on examples of matter being unable to create mind. But interpreting the mind–matter relationship in such a way would be to assume as true the very claim that is in dispute. The same point holds for the claim that no effect is "higher" or "greater" than its cause. This may or may not be true in the material world, but how can we claim to know that it is true of the relation between matter and mind without having assumed what is to be proved?

The theist claims that it is simply inconceivable for mind to have originated from matter. Is the theist's alternative any better in this respect than other available theories? How would God create a mind? Would He make it out of matter? How is this more conceivable than matter originating mind? Would He create it from nothing? This seems even harder to imagine. Would He make it out of Himself? How can we imagine that? God would have to be a person who has bits and pieces of His mind breaking off and turning into little persons. But this would be to think in terms of material analogies: cells dividing. A mind is not like that. A cell can be broken up into parts which can exist independently of it. But thoughts, feelings, and perceptions floating free from the mind to which they belong are inconceivable. Could a thought—e.g., that tomorrow is Monday—just exist floating around by itself, totally unattached to any mind? In order to be capable of "splitting off" to form another mind, mental constituents must be to some extent independent of it. But they are not! A mind's "parts" are as dependent upon it as it is upon them. In summary, it is just as inconceivable that God created minds as it is that matter created them.

We could grant the existence of souls and even contend that they are not created by matter, but this would still fail as evidence that God exists. We could suppose that, just as the ultimate particles of matter might well have existed forever, unconscious souls have existed forever right along with them. It is no more strange that there should be ultimate particles and souls than that there should be ultimate particles alone. If God existed, there would be just one very great soul which existed forever. Why would this be any more likely than a swarm of minor souls existing forever? We could say that these souls were unconscious but had properties such that when matter formed into brains, the souls would merge with them and become conscious. This kind of behavior is no more odd than hydrogen and oxygen atoms having the right properties to form water when combined. (Remember the argument in the section "God and the Laws of Nature." There is no reason to believe that the orderly behavior of things is derived from mind. Even the correlations between brain states and soul states could be ordered naturally.) Must we consider it strange that this kind of potential existed in souls and matter? It is no more strange than the claim that God should have the potential to create the universe. We have to suppose that the potential to form the present state of the world existed somewhere, if not in matter and souls, then in God.

VIII. God and Miracles

It is sometimes argued that if miracles have happened, there must be a God who performed them. The theist considers the presence of miracles to be the direct result of God's mind acting on matter. Now if a Divine mind can act directly on matter to produce miraculous effects, there is no reason to assume the human mind cannot do so. In both cases, minds would be involved. The theist may claim that God's mind is different from the human mind in that only the former has the power to perform miracles. But to make this claim would be to assume the truth of the very point that is to be established. The theist's claim could not be established on the evidence available. The presence of miracles can be used as evidence that some human minds have the power to perform them. This would be as reasonable as believing miracles to be evidence that God's mind has the power to perform them. Either of these conclusions could be drawn because the occurrence of miracles does not suggest any one specific source. We do not see a person perform a miracle the way we are able to see him throw a baseball. But then we do not see God performing miracles either. In fact, we do not *see* God at all. In this argument his very existence is inferred merely from the presence of miracles.

It is here that the theory claiming human beings as the cause of miracles demonstrates its superiority over the theistic theory. Human minds are known to exist, but the existence of God's mind is in dispute. It is more reasonable to assume that when someone desires a miracle, and a miraculous-seeming event occurs, it does so not because of God's help but because the person did it himself. We may not be able to specify in detail how the person's desire for a miracle can help to bring it about, but we are equally unable to specify how God's desire for a miracle can produce one. In both theories, the direct action of a mind on matter is claimed. On this score whatever problem or strong point one theory has the other will have also. But in the theistic theory a further claim is made: that a miracle-working God exists. It is this claim that renders the theistic theory less adequate than the position of the atheist.

Generally speaking, explanations which take as little for granted as possible should always be preferred. If, for example, in a controlled experiment, interferon is administered to cancer patients and this is followed by regression of tumors, only one explanation offers the best account of such a state of affairs. Surely intelligent people would not accept the view that some cancer fairy—a relative of the tooth fairy—has spirited portions of the tumor away because fairies of this type like to be around interferon. The results should be attributed to the interferon—which we *know* exists—and not to the cancer fairy, whose existence is only imagined.

The parallel with the case of God working miracles should be obvious. Perhaps we do not know how interferon works to cause tumor regression but we do know that when it is introduced, tumors regress. Similarly, we may not know how a human being's mind can produce a desired miracle but we may find that when he desires a miracle it occurs. In neither case should we introduce imaginary beings to explain effects which we could just as easily explain by claiming that already existing beings were responsible for them. We should especially avoid such fantasies if we find that they do not assist us to acquire a better understanding of how the effect was brought about than could be obtained with some non-fantasy theory.[31]

The same conclusion can be defended from a different perspective. A miracle must be an event the occurrence of which can be imagined but is nevertheless physically impossible, like pure water catching on fire. Now suppose a Christian argues that we should believe Jesus walked on water, although such a walk is physically impossible. An atheist could agree that Jesus walked on water and yet assert that Jesus was merely a strange sort of freak with an odd talent for walking on water; no god had anything to do with it. The only criticism Christians could offer would be that the existence of such freaks is physically impossible. But this criticism would be self-contradictory. The Christian has already admitted that impossible things of this type can happen when he asserted that Jesus walked on water. On the one hand, Christians claim that physical impossibility does not exclude belief; and yet, when evaluating the beliefs of others, they claim that it does exclude belief.[32] Will it do to claim that only God can make it possible for someone to walk on water? The atheist can reply that, as far as his very unusual freak is concerned, walking on water is possible. As long as we are in the business of offering "explanations" in terms of guessing *who* performed a certain act, with no precise reference as to *how* it was done, we can easily say that *anybody* did it.

The reason why a "miracle" must be physically impossible has to do with the meaning we give the term when we use it. 'Miracles' are defined as events which natural causes, by themselves, could not bring about. It is the impossibility of these events coupled with their existence that leads people to claim God's will to be at work. A serious problem arises, however, because we are unable to identify the limits of natural causes. We learn the capabilities of natural causes only by observing their behavior. There is no other way to learn them. We could, of course, claim to have some instinctive knowledge about how things should naturally behave, but we must be sure this instinctive "knowledge" is correct. The only available means of verifying this knowledge would consist of a comparison with actual situations—observations of natural behavior. If we do not check our conclusions, then our instinctive knowledge would just be unverified guesswork. However, if we do check our knowledge against the actual behavior of nature, then our powers of observation become the final arbiter of what is, in fact, natural behavior. It is ultimately observation, then, that provides us with knowledge of how nature works. Our conception of the powers and capacities of nature is based upon our observation of how nature behaves. For example, we know that the action of gravity is a capacity of matter because we observe that objects tend to fall. A "miracle" would be an observed event, and, as such, would therefore have to count as one small bit of behavior which helps to determine the capacities of nature. If an alleged miraculous event must help to set the limits of what is considered natural behavior, it cannot be claimed to exceed those limits. If an event establishes a rule, it cannot be said to break the rule. Is the theist like a man who says that all swans are white and when shown a black swan admits that it is black but still holds that all swans are white?[33]

This reasoning has been challenged by theists. They point out that, if an event is to be considered the result of natural causes, it must be repeatable. That is, when particular natural causes are present, the event must occur — and it must occur every time these causes are present. Now it is possible that an event might occur which could not be repeated no matter what combination of natural causes were present. Such a natural, nonrepeatable event would have to be considered something beyond the capacities of nature.[34]

The reply is obvious. Suppose I am wandering around an old house and I hear a creaking sound. I theorize that the creaking has been caused by my stepping on a loose plank. How do I confirm this? Simply by stepping on the plank again to see if the creaking sound repeats. In order reasonably to regard an event as the result of a particular cause, we must find that the cause–effect sequence is repeatable. If it could never be repeated, how could we know the supposed cause was the real cause? Now suppose that Jesus walked on water. This event is either repeatable or it is not. If it is not repeatable, then it cannot reasonably be believed to have been caused by Jesus or any other particular agent. If, on the other hand, it is repeatable, then we can indeed claim that Jesus caused it to happen. But the event — being repeatable — will now justify us in revising our conception of the capacities of natural causes. Now we do not see God causing the event. Since the *observable* cause–effect sequence consists of a man — Jesus — walking on water, we must revise our concept of the powers of nature so that we believe it is natural for a mind with certain characteristics and under certain conditions to wish to have its body walk on water, and succeed. An event must be repeatable in the context of observed, natural causes in order for it to be considered the result of any cause. An invisible God producing a naturally nonrepeatable event would bring about a situation equal to a floorboard creaking with no determinable cause.[35]

Another problem with the theist's objection is that an event may be repeatable under certain conditions; but if these conditions never recur, the event may not in fact repeat. The mere fact that an event has not been repeated is no indication that it is not repeatable. It may just be the case that we are unable to reconstruct the conditions under which it is repeatable. For example, under normal circumstances, iron does not attract iron any more than wood attracts wood. But under exceptional circumstances, when iron is magnetized, it does attract iron. The problem for the theist, then, is to distinguish between cases in which an event is not repeatable, and those cases in which it is repeatable but we are not yet able to reconstruct the requisite conditions. The way to go about making this distinction is to investigate the conditions under which the event occurred. But this is impossible since such events often happened long ago. If it is impossible to make the distinction—i.e., impossible to solve the problem—then it would be dishonest to classify the event as anything but an unsolved problem. Nor would classifying it as an unsolved problem distort our conception of the relevant laws of nature. We would not be classifying the event as part of the natural order; we would simply be suspending judgment on it. Certainly it would be unwarrantable to classify such a state of affairs as a miracle.

The preceding discussion assumes we have good evidence that so-called miraculous events have happened. However, the requirements for such evidence must be very strict. The most reliable testimony for the occurrence of an event is found in situations where it is contrary to our expectations that the testimony could be false. For example, if a man claims that an event occurred even when he is threatened with torture for making such a claim, it would be contrary to our expectations to believe that anyone in these circumstances would lie. We would then have strong reasons to believe that the man was not lying. But suppose that the event in question is a miracle. It too would be contrary to our expectations. If we do not believe that lying was involved, since it would be contrary to our expectations, then we must also disbelieve that the miracle occurred because it too is contrary to expectations. If being contrary to our expectations is reason for disbelief in the one case, it must be so in the other. Whatever reason we can offer in favor of belief in testimony to the miraculous is automatically opposed by the assumptions we have to make about miracles.[36]

Objections to this simple reasoning have not been lacking. For example, it could be said that miracles are not contrary to our expectations. No one would doubt that if an ordinary man died of cancer, it would be contrary to our expectations for him to come back to life. The theist could insist that the case of, say, Jesus's resurrection was different, because Jesus was the Son of God and it is not contrary to our expectations that the Son of God should rise from the dead. But this tactic just assumes what the theist is trying to prove. If miracles are to be the proof that Jesus was the Son of God, then obviously the belief that Jesus was the Son of God cannot be used to help prove the miracles. If the conclusion of an argument has not yet been reached, we cannot use the conclusion to help us reach it. I am no more assuming that Jesus was not the Son of God, than I would assume that anyone I had just met is not the Son of God. I presume that each person I meet is a normal, ordinary human being until proven otherwise. That a stranger might actually be a man from Mars or the Son of God is not considered an open question.

The rule requiring greater evidence as a testament to the miraculous is certainly supported by common sense. If I tell you that I jumped two feet off the ground, you would believe me as a matter of course. But if I told you I had jumped one hundred, you would demand a considerable amount of evidence before assenting to my claim. It may be objected that following this rule occasionally forces us to disbelieve actual happenings. Perhaps so, but this does not mean that we must not follow the rule. For if we follow it, we will more likely be right than wrong. If we do not follow it, we will suffer for our gullibility.

IX. God and Religious Experience

There are theists who say they do not need to offer arguments for God's existence because they experience Him directly. What precisely is meant by this "experience"? It is either similar to ordinary sense experience (i.e., seeing, hearing, and the like) or it is not. Let us consider first the possibility that it resembles ordinary sense experience. This would be the strongest position for the theist to take because we generally trust our senses. Let us suppose there is an isolated group of people who occasionally experience a feeling which they describe as "a devil hitting the inside of my head." Would this experience tend to prove that there were in fact devils inside their heads? Or does the phrase 'a devil hitting the inside of my head' simply describe a feeling that could just as easily have been described by the word 'headache'? This example demonstrates the problems we encounter in ascribing otherwise unverifiable causes to experiences which are private to each individual.[37]

In response to the above example, a theist might point out that we would normally believe a friend's claim that he had seen a wolf in the woods. Therefore, we should believe him if he claims to have encountered God. Of course, his claim to have seen a wolf would be based on his eyesight — and we would first have to know if his eyesight is reliable. We would not want to believe an eyewitness's visual report if we knew him to be nearly blind. Furthermore, our person who says he saw the wolf should be able to tell the difference between photographs of dogs and those of wolves. We would not trust someone's report if he could not tell a wolf from a dog. If the theist's experience of God is like sense experience, then how do we know that the theist is not like a nearly blind man who is unable to distinguish wolves from dogs? To know that the religious sense is reliable, we would have to test it to see if it could be used to tell the difference between gods and other types of things a theist might be sensing instead. The reliability of our eyesight is tested every day. If we do not walk into walls or over furniture, and if we are capable of distinguishing one person from another, then our eyesight is considered reliable. But how do we test this supposed religious sense? We would have to already know that God exists before we could find that the religious sense was reliable in detecting him. This is because a test would consist of discovering whether God was in fact near when a theist sensed His presence. And to know this we would have to have some independent means of knowing that God exists.[38]

Now let us consider the possibility that religious experience is not like ordinary sense experience. We know the conditions under which ordinary sense experience is considered reliable. But how do we know that God–experiences are at least as reliable as these sense experiences? We have no way of knowing that an "intuition" of God accurately confirms His existence. To test such an intuitive "sense" we would have to demonstrate that whenever we have an intuition of God's existence, God in fact does exist. But in order to show this, we would have to have an additional intuition. A further, independent intuition of His existence could not serve to confirm the accuracy of the first kind of intuition because it too would have to be confirmed for exactly the same reasons.

In summary, either religious experience is like ordinary sense experience or else it is not. If it is not, we have no way to test whether it is as reliable as sense experience. If it is like ordinary sense experience, then we have no way of testing its accuracy without assuming God's existence independently of the evidence.

X. God and Morality

Where do we obtain our knowledge of what is good and evil? The theist may claim that what is in fact good or evil must be independent of human opinion. If it were not, the majority would determine good and evil, and majority opinion can change. But we know that good and evil do not change with human opinion. Therefore it must depend on God's commands.

While we certainly are of the mind that the content of good and evil do not change with majority opinion, we also feel that they do not change with God's commands. Suppose God commanded that lying, stealing, and murdering were now our moral duty. Does anyone seriously believe that these actions would somehow become morally good? Whether or not God would command such things is beside the point. It must be made clear that *if* he did, this would not make them good.

The theist's theory of morality cannot explain why we

have a moral obligation to obey God's commands. For if all moral obligations originate from God's commands, then our moral obligation to obey these commands must also originate from a command by God—namely, a command to obey his commands. But if this is the case, then no moral reason has been offered for obeying *this* command. We would have to say that the moral duty to obey God's commands must result from an even more prior command, one that compels us to obey his commands. But, then, why should we obey *this* command? It is plain that we will get nowhere by grounding moral obligation on God's commands alone.[39]

Suppose we are told that we have a moral obligation to obey God's commands because we love God. But this implies that we *ought* to love God. Why ought we to do so? Because God commands it? But if we take this course, we must contend with the same difficulties detailed above. Should we love and/or obey God because he is good? But 'good' as used here could mean only one of two things. First, we could mean that "good" is only what God commands—and we are back to our previous difficulties. Second, we could mean that God's goodness is independent of his commands. If so, what is good does not depend on what God commands. And this is, of course, the point I have been attempting to make.

It is sometimes argued that God is the standard of what is "good." 'Goodness' has no meaning apart from its existence in God. But we would have to know independently of God what 'goodness' is before we could use him as its standard. This is because we must be able to pick out from among God's other qualities his quality of goodness. If we did not already know what 'goodness' is, how could we differentiate it from among God's other qualities? We might instead pick out his power and use that as an example of "goodness." Compare this case with that of a yardstick. It is a yard long, and three feet are marked off. It is a standard of length. From it, we can tell *how long* something is but not what 'length' itself is. We must already know what 'length' is, otherwise we would not know how to use the yardstick. (If the yardstick were white, for example, we might mistakenly use it as the standard of "length" under the impression that "whiteness" was what is called 'length.') If we must know what 'goodness' is *before* God can be used as its standard, we can judge whether or not God has this quality of "goodness." This, of course, means that we possess knowledge of "goodness" which is independent of God.[40]

Either specific moral rules are good independently of God's approval or else they are good merely because God approves them. If they are good independently of God's approval, then moral standards do not originate with God, and the extent of God's conformity to them can be judged. If, on the other hand, moral rules are good merely because God approves of them, then God cannot really be called good. This is because 'goodness' would mean "being approved by God." The statement that God is "good" would mean only that God "approves" of God. And this is not what we typically mean in saying that God is good. Under this definition, "good" would be determined by God's non-moral characteristics. God could will that lying, stealing, and murdering are good. Satan could continue to oppose God, and hold that lying, stealing, and murdering are wrong and to be avoided. And we would have to continue to hold that God is good and Satan is evil.[41] But in believing this, we have emptied the term 'good' of all meaning.

Consider a parallel case. Suppose I keep claiming that John has long hair regardless of whether he has grown it out to two feet, trimmed it to four inches, or shaved it to the scalp. My use of the word 'long' as applied to John's hair will have become meaningless because it has no meaningful contrast. If I count nothing as short hair where John is concerned, then when I discuss the length of his hair no one hearing me will credit anything I say on the subject with being informative. Suppose you have been out of town for six months and I told you that John's hair is long. You would have no idea whether I meant it was shaved to the scalp or a foot long. Similarly, if I call God's conduct "good" no matter what he does, no one would believe that I am saying anything more than that God's conduct is God's conduct. The word 'good' will not be informative and therefore, when joined with the word 'conduct,' will tell us no more than the word 'conduct' by itself.

The obvious conclusion is that if the meaning of 'good' is determined by God's wishes, then the word 'good' when applied to God is meaningless (i.e., provides no information about God whatsoever). And this is the equivalent of saying that God is not good. Therefore, either there are moral standards independent of God's will or else God is not good.

It will not do to object that God would not approve of acts such as murder because he possesses such characteristics as love and respect for justice. For this would be to admit that there are standards independent of God's arbitrary approval. And since we know what love and respect for justice imply, we would know what kind of behavior in God would exemplify it. We could therefore judge whether God conforms to these standards. But if we cannot judge whether God, in any particular case, has acted in conformity with these standards, then there is no way we can be assured that God will not approve murder and other terrible actions. Therefore love and respect for justice must be moral standards to which God is expected to conform, otherwise we are back to our original situation: God could approve murder and we would have to call it good.

Let us suppose that there was an evil Creator who created moral rules and commanded us to do what the rules specified even though the actions are evil. Since this case is perfectly parallel to that of God, we would have to say that this evil Creator's will defined what is *evil*. But if so, how would we differentiate this evil Creator from the Christian Creator who established moral rules and commanded us to do the *good* actions they require? Either there is a difference or there is not. If there is a difference, then it can only be in words, for the Creators might change their minds — the evil Creator deciding to recommend what was previously labelled 'good' and the Christian Creator deciding to recommend what had been called 'evil.' Although the actions recommended would in both cases be quite different, the labels 'good' and 'evil' would be swapped so that the evil Creator's will would still define "evil" and the Christian Creator's will would still define "good." The difference between the two Creators must be a matter of words only, if there is any difference at all. On the other hand, if it is admitted that there is no difference between the good Creator and the evil Creator, then we see that it is nonsense to call God "good" if His will defines what is good. At *most,* there can only be a verbal difference. Therefore, it is nonsense to call God "good" regardless of what alternative is taken.

It is sometimes suggested that God has supreme moral *authority;* His will and morality are so closely related that his will is the only *justification* for morality. An adult is more knowledgeable than a child and therefore more authoritative. God must therefore be the most authoritative of all. But even if we grant God's existence it does not follow that God's will is the only justification for morality. We would have to know that God's will is good independently of his authoritative judgments. Otherwise we would have no way to reply to the objection that differences in our judgment and God's judgment may result from God's lack of goodness rather than from our lack of knowledge. We must be able to rule out this alternative by knowing that God is good independently of his judgments. And to do this we would have to be able to judge, independently of God's authoritative judgments, that in many instances his judgments are morally right. But to grant that we can do this would be to admit that God's authoritative judgments are not in all cases the last word, for we must judge them. It follows that morality must be independent of God's authority.[42]

It may be said that our moral judgment is completely corrupt, therefore we must rely on God. But if our moral judgment is so corrupt, then we cannot rely on it when we judge that God is morally reliable. Furthermore, an unreliable moral judgment will not even be able to identify what *is* God's will from among many rival claims concerning the substance of that will.[43]

XI. God and Faith

The theist, whose reasons for believing in God have thus far been demolished, often resorts to faith. But even faith is a weak support. We are told that ultimately nothing can be proven true and that consequently we must rely on faith throughout our lives. For example, we have faith that the floor will not disappear beneath us. We are unable to prove that the floor will not simply vanish, yet we nonetheless believe that it will remain. Why, then, do we need to prove that God exists?

Suppose a man claimed that there are ten fairies on Mars or that George Washington is alive today. It would not be reasonable for him to retort, when asked for evidence in support of these claims: "Well, what evidence do you have that the floor will not disappear beneath you?" From this example, we can draw the conclusion that common-sense beliefs – e.g., that the floor will not vanish – are much more rationally supported than beliefs for which we have no evidence. Common-sense beliefs and belief in God are therefore not comparable.[44] In our everyday lives we certainly act upon assumptions which we cannot *prove* to be true. But we nevertheless decide what to do on the basis of what is most probably true. We would be fools if we did not.

Consider the problem of stepping out of a window 1,000 feet above the ground. We could have faith that we will fall and be killed or we could have faith that we will walk on the air. Faith can decide nothing here. And yet we do have good reasons to decide not to step out of that window. No reasonable person would claim that we do not.

The theist argues that we have to rely on some faith in our everyday lives and then, using this statement as a spring board, he leaps to the conclusion that faith in anything is somehow justified — fairies, leprechauns, walking on air, and God. But the fact remains that we do not have good reasons for believing any of these things. Faith or not, proof or not — we still have to decide on the basis of whether there are good reasons available for our beliefs. Whether or not good reasons are "proofs," they will at least do until proofs come along. The question still remains: do we have good reasons for believing in God?

We do have good reasons for accepting common-sense beliefs. We have *observed* that certain things have happened in the past and we *assume* that they will continue to occur — floors will remain in place, and the like. Theistic claims are based merely on *assumption,* whereas common-sense beliefs are based on assumption preceded by *observation.* Theistic claims are therefore less justified than common-sense beliefs.

Beyond the above point, we should note that common-sense belief is presupposed by theistic beliefs. For example,

I must hold the common-sense belief that there exist things other than myself in order for me to believe that there exists a God. I must believe that what is true in the past will continue to be true, if I am to believe, from split-second to split-second, that God continues to exist. Common-sense beliefs are more fundamental than theistic beliefs. Therefore, if common-sense beliefs are unjustified, then theistic beliefs are doubly unjustified since they rest on common-sense beliefs. If two unjustified assumptions are no worse than one, then we could permit an unlimited number of unjustified assumptions. But this is just a blueprint for non-rational belief.[45]

It is sometimes argued that we have a fifty-fifty betting proposition when considering God's existence or nonexistence. If we bet that God exists and he does exist, then we lose nothing while possibly gaining salvation. If we bet that God exists and he does not exist, then we lose nothing. But if we bet that God does not exist and he *does* exist, then we lose everything. Of course, if we bet that God does not exist and we are correct, then we lose nothing. Therefore, it is prudent to bet on God.[46]

The problem with the above argument is that it does not establish a fifty-fifty betting proposition. There are many alternatives that it fails to consider. For example, God may exist but he may damn anyone who "bets" on his existence merely for reasons of prudence. He may consider such a "bet" to be an insult. Furthermore, it may be that a mere belief in God is not enough to ensure salvation. A further requirement may be the belief in a particular religion. But *which* religion? Again, there are many alternatives. Another possible alternative is that God offers salvation only to atheists because God does not like being surrounded by obsequious "yes-men." God may prize independence and skepticism.

XII. God and the Problem of Evil

Here is a common situation: a house catches on fire and a six-month-old baby is painfully burned to death. Could we possibly describe as "good" any person who had the power to save this child and yet refused to do so? God undoubtedly has this power and yet in many cases of this sort he has refused to help. Can we call God "good"? Are there adequate excuses for his behavior?

First, it will not do to claim that the baby will go to heaven. It was either necessary for the baby to suffer or it was not. If it was not, then it was wrong to allow it. The child's ascent to heaven does not change this fact. If it was necessary, the fact that the baby will go to heaven does not explain why it was necessary, and we are still left without an excuse for God's inaction.

It is not enough to say that the baby's painful death would in the long run have good results and therefore should have happened, otherwise God would not have

99

permitted it. For if we know this to be true, then we know — just as God knows — that every action successfully performed must in the end be good and therefore the right thing to do, otherwise God would not have allowed it to happen. We could deliberately set houses ablaze to kill innocent people and if successful we would then know we had a duty to do it. A defense of God's goodness which takes as its foundation duties known only after the fact would result in a morality unworthy of the name. Furthermore, this argument does not explain why God allowed the child to burn to death. It merely claims that there is some reason discoverable in the long run. But the belief that such a reason is within our grasp must rest upon the additional belief that God is good. This is just to counter evidence against such a belief by assuming the belief to be true. It is not unlike a lawyer defending his client by claiming that the client is innocent and therefore the evidence against him must be misleading — that proof vindicating the defendant will be found in the long run. No jury of reasonable men and women would accept such a defense and the theist cannot expect a more favorable outcome.

The theist often claims that man has been given free will so that if he accidentally or purposefully causes fires, killing small children, it is his fault alone. Consider a bystander who had nothing to do with starting the fire but who refused to help even though he could have saved the child with no harm to himself. Could such a bystander be called good? Certainly not. If we would not consider a mortal human being good under these circumstances, what grounds could we possibly have for continuing to assert the goodness of an all-powerful God?

The suggestion is sometimes made that it is best for us to face disasters without assistance, otherwise we would become dependent on an outside power for aid. Should we then abolish modern medical care or do away with efficient fire departments? Are we not dependent on their help? Is it not the case that their presence transforms us into soft, dependent creatures? The vast majority are not physicians or firemen. These people help in their capacity as professional outside sources of aid in much the same way that we would expect God to be helpful. Theists refer to aid from firemen and physicians as cases of man helping himself. In reality, it is a tiny minority of men helping a great many. We can become just as dependent on them as we can on God. Now the existence of this kind of outside help is either wrong or right. If it is right, then God should assist those areas of the world which do not have this kind of help. In fact, throughout history, such help has not been available. If aid ought to have been provided, then God should have provided it. On the other hand, if it is wrong to provide this kind of assistance, then we should abolish the aid altogether. But we obviously do not believe it is wrong.

Similar considerations apply to the claim that if God interferes in disasters, he would destroy a considerable amount of moral urgency to make things right. Once again, note that such institutions as modern medicine and fire departments are relatively recent. They function irrespective of whether we as individuals feel any moral urgency to support them. To the extent that they help others, opportunities to feel moral urgency are destroyed because they reduce the number of cases which appeal to us for help. Since we have not always had such institutions, there must have been a time when there was greater moral urgency than there is now. If such a situation is morally desirable, then we should abolish modern medical care and fire departments. If the situation is not morally desirable, then God should have remedied it.

Besides this point, we should note that God is represented as one who tolerates disasters, such as infants burning to death, in order to create moral urgency. It follows that God approves of these disasters as a means to encourage the creation of moral urgency. Furthermore, if there were no such disasters occurring, God would have to see to it that they occur. If it so happened that we lived in a world in which babies never perished in burning houses, God would be morally obliged to take an active hand in setting fire to houses with infants in them. In fact, if the frequency of infant mortality due to fire should happen to fall below a level necessary for the creation of maximum moral urgency in our real world, God would be justified in setting a few fires of his own. This may well be happening right now, for there is no guarantee that the maximum number of infant deaths necessary for moral urgency are occurring.

All of this is of course absurd. If I see an opportunity to create otherwise nonexistent opportunities for moral urgency by burning an infant or two, then I should *not* do so. But if it is good to maximize moral urgency, then I *should* do so. Therefore, it is not good to maximize moral urgency. Plainly we do not in general believe that it is a good thing to maximize moral urgency. The fact that we approve of modern medical care and applaud medical advances is proof enough of this.

The theist may point out that in a world without suffering there would be no occasion for the production of such virtues as courage, sympathy, and the like. This may be true, but the atheist need not demand a world without suffering. He need only claim that there is suffering which is in excess of that needed for the production of various virtues. For example, God's active attempts to save six-month-old infants from fires would not in itself create a world without suffering. But no one could sincerely doubt that it would improve the world.

The two arguments against the previous theistic excuse apply here also. "Moral urgency" and "building virtue" are susceptible to the same criticisms. It is worthwhile to emphasize, however, that we encourage efforts to eliminate evils; we approve of efforts to promote peace, prevent famine, and wipe out disease. In other words, we do value a world with fewer or (if possible) no opportunities for the development of virtue (when "virtue" is understood to mean the reduction of suffering). If we produce such a world for succeeding generations, how will they develop virtues? Without war, disease, and famine, they will not be virtuous. Should we then cease our attempts to wipe out war, disease, and famine? If we do not believe that it is right to cease attempts at improving the world, then by implication we admit that virtue-building is not an excuse for God to permit disasters. For we admit that the development of virtue is no excuse for permitting disasters.

It might be said that God allows innocent people to suffer in order to deflate man's ego so that the latter will not be proud of his apparently deserved good fortune. But this excuse succumbs to the arguments used against the preceding excuses and we need discuss them no further.

Theists may claim that evil is a necessary by-product of the laws of nature and therefore it is irrational for God to interfere every time a disaster happens. Such a state of affairs would alter the whole causal order and we would then find it impossible to predict anything. But the death of a child caused by an electrical fire could have been prevented by a miracle and no one would ever have known. Only a minor alteration in electrical equipment would have been necessary. A very large disaster could have been avoided simply by producing in Hitler a miraculous heart attack — and no one would have known it was a miracle. To argue that continued miraculous intervention by God would be wrong is like insisting that one should never use salt because ingesting five pounds of it would be fatal. No one is requesting that God interfere all of the time. He should, however, intervene to prevent especially horrible disasters. Of course, the question arises: where does one draw the line? Well, certainly the line should be drawn somewhere this side of infants burning to death. To argue that we do not know where the line should be drawn is no excuse for failing to interfere in those instances that would be called clear cases of evil.

It will not do to claim that evil exists as a necessary contrast to good so that we might know what good is. A very small amount of evil, such as a toothache, would allow that. It is not necessary to destroy innocent human beings.

The claim could be made that God has a "higher morality" by which his actions are to be judged. But it is a strange "higher morality" which claims that what we call "bad" is good and what we call "good" is bad. Such a morality can have no meaning to us. It would be like calling black "white" and white "black." In reply the theist may say that God is the wise Father and we are ignorant children. How can we judge God any more than a child is able to judge his parent? It is true that a child may be puzzled by his parents' conduct, but his basis for deciding that their conduct is nevertheless good would be the many instances of good behavior he has observed. Even so, this could be misleading. Hitler, by all accounts, loved animals and children of the proper race; but if Hitler had had a child, this offspring would hardly have been justified in arguing that his father was a good man. At any rate, God's "higher morality," being the opposite of ours, cannot offer any grounds for deciding that he is somehow good.

Perhaps the main problem with the solutions to the problem of evil we have thus far considered is that no matter how convincing they may be in the abstract, they are implausible in certain particular cases. Picture an infant dying in a burning house and then imagine God simply observing from afar. Perhaps God is reciting excuses in his own behalf. As the child succumbs to the smoke and flames, God may be pictured as saying: "Sorry, but if I helped you I would have considerable trouble deflating the ego of your parents. And don't forget I have to keep those laws of nature consistent. And anyway if you weren't dying in that fire, a lot of moral urgency would just go down the drain. Besides, I didn't start this fire, so you can't blame *me*."

It does no good to assert that God may not be all-powerful and thus not able to prevent evil. He can create a universe and yet is conveniently unable to do what the fire department can do — rescue a baby from a burning building. God should at least be as powerful as a man. A man, if he had been at the right place and time, could have killed Hitler. Was this beyond God's abilities? If God knew in 1910 how to produce polio vaccine and if he was able to communicate with somebody, he should have communicated this knowledge. He must be incredibly limited if he could not have managed this modest accomplishment. Such a God if not dead, is the next thing to it. And a person who believes in such a ghost of a God is practically an atheist. To call such a thing a god would be to strain the meaning of the word.

The theist, as usual, may retreat to faith. He may say that he has faith in God's goodness and therefore the Christian Deity's existence has not been disproved. "Faith" is here understood as being much like confidence in a friend's innocence despite the evidence against him. Now in order to have confidence in a friend one must know him well enough to justify faith in his goodness. We cannot have justifiable faith in the supreme goodness of strangers. Moreover, such confidence must come not just from a speaking acquaintance. The friend may continually assure us with his words that he is good but if he does not act like a good person, we would have no reason to trust him. A person who says he has faith in God's goodness is speaking as if he had known God for a long time and during that time had never seen Him do any serious evil. But we know that throughout history God has allowed numerous atrocities to occur. No one can have justifiable faith in the goodness of such a God. This faith would have to be based on a close friendship wherein God was never found to do anything wrong. But a person would have to be blind and deaf to have had such a relationship with God. Suppose a friend of yours had always claimed to be good yet refused to help people when he was in a position to render aid. Could you have justifiable faith in his goodness?

You can of course say that you trust God anyway—that no arguments can undermine your faith. But this is just a statement describing how stubborn you are; it has no bearing whatsoever on the question of God's goodness.

The various excuses theists offer for why God has allowed evil to exist have been demonstrated to be inadequate. However, the conclusive objection to these excuses does not depend on their inadequacy.

First, we should note that every possible excuse making the actual world consistent with the existence of a good God could be used in reverse to make that same world consistent with an evil God. For example, we could say that God is evil and that he allows free will so that we can freely do evil things, which would make us more truly evil than we would be if forced to perform evil acts. Or we could say that natural disasters occur in order to make people more selfish and bitter, for most people tend to have a "me-first" attitude in a disaster (note, for example, stampedes to leave burning buildings). Even though some people achieve virtue from disasters, this outcome is necessary if persons are to react freely to disaster—necessary if the development of moral degeneracy is to continue freely. But, enough; the point is made. Every excuse we could provide to make the world consistent with a good God can be paralleled by an excuse to make the world consistent with an evil God. This is so because the world is a mixture of both good and bad.

Now there are only three possibilities concerning God's moral character. Considering the world as it actually is, we may believe: (*a*) that God is more likely to be all evil than he is to be all good; (*b*) that God is less likely to be all evil than he is to be all good; or (*c*) that God is equally as likely to be all evil as he is to be all good. In case (*a*) it would be admitted that God is unlikely to be all good. Case (*b*) cannot be true at all, since—as we have seen—the belief that God is all evil can be justified to precisely the same extent as the belief that God is all good. Case (*c*) leaves us with no reasonable excuses for a good God to permit evil. The reason is as follows: if an excuse is to be a reasonable excuse, the circumstances it identifies as excusing conditions must be actual. For example, if I run over a pedestrian and my excuse is that the brakes failed because someone tampered with them, then the facts had better bear this out. Otherwise the excuse will not hold. Now if case (c) is correct and, given the facts of the actual world, God is as likely to be all evil as he is to be all good, then these facts do not support the excuses which could be made for a good God permitting evil. Consider an analogous example. If my excuse for running over the pedestrian is that my brakes were tampered with, and if the actual facts lead us to believe that it is no more likely that they were tampered with than that they were not, the excuse is no longer reasonable. To make good my excuse, I must show that it is a fact or at least highly probable that my brakes were tampered with — not that it is just a possibility. The same point holds for God. His excuse must not be a possible excuse, but an actual one. But case (c), in maintaining that it is just as likely that God is all evil as that he is all good, rules this out. For if case (c) is true, then the facts of the actual world do not make it any more likely that God is all good than that he is all evil. Therefore, they do not make it any more likely that his excuses are good than that they are not. But, as we have seen, good excuses have a higher probability of being true.

Cases (a) and (c) conclude that it is unlikely that God is all good, and case (b) cannot be true. Since these are the only possible cases, there is no escape from the conclusion that it is unlikely that God is all good. Thus the problem of evil triumphs over traditional theism.[47]

XIII. God and Christianity

Having discussed theism in general, we may now turn our attention briefly to a prominent example of theism: Christianity. Here we will see theism in action and examine some of the moral absurdities it appears to encourage. In order to criticize the moral content of Christian beliefs we must first deal with the objection that we cannot judge God. With that defense out of the way, we can range at will through Christian beliefs and expose them as morally inadequate.

First, in criticizing Christian beliefs, we are not judging God; we are judging what Christians say about God. If it is wrong to object to the claims people make about God, then anyone could claim that God approves of mass murder and no one would have a right to criticize this claim as unworthy of the Deity. Before we can be accused of judging God's behavior, we must first know that his alleged behavior is *in fact* his behavior. If I criticize a man for falsely claiming that my friend beat his wife, I am not criticizing my friend for beating his wife. I am criticizing the man who lied about his behavior. Similarly, if I criticize Christians for claiming that God behaves in what I believe to be an evil manner, then I am not judging God — I am judging Christians. The issue here is whether God's actions are what Christians claim them to be. If I charge that God is too good to engage in behavior which I believe to be immoral, then it will not do for Christians to respond that I am judging God. For this would be simply to assume the point which is at issue: namely, that God in fact does these things.

Second, no Christian can afford to claim that we cannot judge God. If God creates the rules by which behavior must be judged and if the rules do not bind their Creator, then there is nothing that is improper for God. Therefore, when God promises that Christians will go to heaven and atheists will go to hell, there is no reason to believe that he will not break his promise and send Christians to hell and atheists to heaven. In fact, it is just as likely that he will break his promise as it is that he will not. What possible grounds could the Christian have for maintaining that God will keep the promise in question? God's love for Christians? But we could not call him unloving if he sent Christians to hell, for this would be to judge God. Could we say that God will keep his promise because he is honorable? But again, if God broke his promises we could not judge him to be dishonorable, for that too would be a judgment. If, then, we must hold that *whatever* God does is the right thing, then we have no way of knowing *what* he will do. The Christian who insists that we cannot judge God is also adhering (although inadvertently) to the belief that Christians will go to heaven is just a guess, and anyone else's guess is just as good. If Christians are right and we cannot judge God, then Christianity is in serious trouble. It is not a religion but, in fact, only a self-confessed haphazard guess.

Third, the claim that we cannot judge God is simply false. It apparently rests on two distinct grounds. The claim is made that God makes the rules and, as the Creator of the rules, he cannot be judged by them, for they are not independent of his wishes. It is also claimed that a creature cannot judge its creator. The first reason is false because, as we demonstrated in the section "God and Morality," moral rules must be independent of God's wishes. The second reason is false because we are discussing morality, and not who created whom. If I created a human being out of nothing, that fact alone would not give me the right to treat him in any way I saw fit. He would be no less a human being for having been my creation. Suppose I were uncreated. This would not change matters. Whether or not *I* was created is irrelevant to whether I am right or wrong in treating *my* creation as I see fit. Creation is not a moral concept, and only a moral concept can give moral authority.

Fourth, to call God good is just as much a judgment of his moral character as saying that he is evil. In the former case we are enthusiastic about what he has done; in the latter case, we are much less so. Whether statements about God are positive or negative evaluations, they share the characteristic of being judgmental. A judge is no less a judge for finding the accused not guilty. A refusal to judge God would be a refusal to commit oneself with respect to His moral character. If I refuse to judge a beauty contest, I am not thereby finding that any particular contestant is most beautiful. That is precisely what I am *not* doing. If I refuse to judge the quality of a student's term paper, I am not thereby giving him an "A." I am simply making no judgment. The Christian equates "judging" with finding fault. But if I judge that a cake you have just baked is excellent I am not finding fault with it. What I *am* doing when I judge a thing is to set myself above it in that I am subjecting it to approval or disapproval as I see fit. But if I approve I am setting myself above that which I judge quite as much as if I had disapproved. If we approve of God, and if this is to mean more than that we simply acknowledge that God approves of God, then we are judging God. The Christian cannot help judging God. If the Christian can do so, there can be no objection to the atheist's doing so.

The fundamentalist's belief in both the blamelessness of God and the reality of hell is inconsistent. God must know that many people in the past have gone to hell. And he must know that if the human race is allowed to continue reproducing itself there will be many more victims, for there is no reason to believe that people will suddenly become completely virtuous. If God knows that this state of affairs will continue, he is responsible for the deliberate production of victims for hell. In effect, God—who created the human race in the first place and who has allowed it to propagate—has created victims in order to flood the gates of hell. There is little difference in allowing people to be created while knowing that in fact they will be damned because of their immoral ways, and creating people for the expressed purpose of damning them. Compare the parallel case of a couple who continue having children. Now if they knew that half the children they are likely to have will probably grow up in horribly miserable conditions, then this couple would be morally blameworthy if they decide to have more children. The plight of these children has been given the implicit approval of their parents. It is as if the children have been produced for the express purpose of being miserable. It will hardly do to object that if the reproduction of human beings is halted by God, this will deprive persons who otherwise would have existed of the chance to go to heaven. One cannot deprive a nonexistent person of anything. There is nobody there to deprive. Compare this situation with the case of a couple who decide not to have any children. Is the unfertilized egg being harmed by this decision?

The Christian God is by definition morally superior to any human being. And God must also know *at least* as much as any human being. But, so defined, God becomes as impossible as a round square. In order to know at least as much as any man, He must know what it is like to feel jealousy or lust. To have full knowledge of these emotions, God must feel them himself—for these are feelings and their existence consists in being felt. But if he feels these emotions himself he would not be morally superior to human beings, for it is precisely these emotions which serve to make us immoral.[48]

To object that God may feel these urges but not give in to them is to miss the point. First, God would not know what it is like to give in to temptation, which is something every human being knows. Second, merely feeling such urges is in itself evidence of an imperfect character. As Jesus Christ said in Matthew 5:28: "Whosoever looketh on a woman to lust after her hath committed adultery with her already in his heart." To object that God may know what these immoral urges are through empathy is also to miss the point. If this were the case, then God would lack direct personal knowledge of them. For God to feel jealousy and lust to a lesser extent than human beings do would mean that He does not know them in precisely the way human beings know them. And this means that there is something human beings know that God does not know. Consequently God does not know at least as much as human beings. Contrary to the definition of God, he cannot at the same time be morally superior to human beings and know at least as much as they do.[49]

The above reasoning has some additional consequences. If we retain God's supreme morality and sacrifice his knowledge, then God has no basis upon which to judge immoral urges in human beings. He does not really know or understand what these urges are because he has not experienced their strength and therefore cannot judge how difficult they are to avoid or resist. In judging human beings, God would be like a blind judge at a beauty contest. On the other hand, if we retain God's knowledge and sacrifice his supreme morality, we find that God is as much to be condemned as anyone else. Both alternatives are unacceptable to Christian theism, yet one of them must be true. Therefore Christian theism cannot rest upon firm foundations.

The Christian belief that Christianity is necessary to salvation is morally unjustifiable. Christianity did not come into being instantaneously all over the world. In fact, it spread rather slowly after the death of Christ, involving missionary work even into the nineteenth century. Since there have been millions who died without ever hearing of Christ, the Christian is confronted with a dilemma. Either these people could be saved or they could not. If they could not, then we are confronted with an obvious example of injustice. Some people were given a chance to be saved, while others were not. The geographical area or historical era in which a person lives does not make any difference in what he deserves. And yet, according to Christianity, people are being treated differently on the basis of factors which do not make any difference in what they deserve. On the other hand, suppose that these people could be saved. Then it follows that the Christian religion is not necessary to salvation. But the fact that Christianity offers salvation is its only excuse for existence, at least according to fundamentalists. Therefore Christianity is worthless. The whole enterprise of sending out missionaries to preach the Gospel has been a foolish waste of time. In fact, if only those who hear and reject the Gospel are damned, then it has imperilled souls rather than saving them.

It will not do to object that everyone deserves damnation so that no one ever actually gets less than he deserves. That is not the question at issue. God's injustice would consist not in the punishment he gives to those who deserve it, but in the fact that he rewards some of the undeserving and punishes the rest. The injustice consists in the undeserved *difference* that is a deciding factor in the treatment of people. If the difference in treatment is undeserved, then it is unjust. A teacher who gives an examination which everyone subsequently fails but who nevertheless gives excellent grades to a few students because they are his favorites constitutes a similar example of injustice.[49]

The existence of hell cannot be justified by reference to the useful effects hell will have on the damned or on others. For the damned will remain in hell forever; no reformation will be of any use to them. And as for the possibility of hell being a deterrent, this effect can be felt without the existence of an actual hell. Since we cannot see hell anyway, only a belief in it is needed to achieve a deterrent effect. Therefore no reform or deterrent theory can justify the actual existence of hell. The only possible justification would be that the damned *deserve* to suffer. But a theory of punishment justified in terms of what is deserved is open to serious question. To say that punishment is deserved implies that moral offense and suffering should go together, because they strike a moral balance. But in that case, if a moral offense justifies suffering, then undeserved suffering justifies the commission of a moral offense. Consider Frank, unjustly imprisoned one year for a robbery he did not commit. When he is released, is he now justified in committing a robbery? He has already paid the penalty and he now deserves to get what he paid for. If suffering should be paired with moral offense, then Frank should now commit a moral offense to balance his suffering. If Frank was unjustly deprived of his freedom, then the only possible restitution is not to deprive him of his freedom in a case where he should be so deprived. But this is absurd. Note that what is absurd is giving Frank what he *deserves*.

To take an even more absurd example, suppose John was in an auto accident and suffered from it exactly as much as Frank suffered from his prison experience. Is John now justified in committing a robbery because he had an auto accident? If suffering and moral offense should be paired because a moral balance can be achieved only in this way, then John is justified in committing the robbery. But clearly he is not so justified. Therefore suffering and moral offense cannot be morally linked.[51] The idea of *deserved* punishment is morally absurd because it leads to ridiculous consequences. But, if so, then the idea of hell is morally absurd. For, as we have seen, hell can only be justified by claiming that the damned *deserve* to suffer.

The theist may object that true punishment can only be applied *after* the moral offense and then only *intentionally*.

But we are discussing here what a person *deserves*. Neither the time of the offense nor the motives of those who inflict the punishment is at all relevant to what the offender *deserves*. If a person has suffered unjustly, then the only possible way to make this right is to allow him not to suffer justly. He *deserves* this restitution.

Human beings cannot be morally responsible to God. If we blame a person for an evil act, we thereby imply that he was to some extent evil prior to his action. For to say that a person is responsible for an evil action is to say that he caused it because he was evil. But how did he *become* evil? If he made himself evil, then this would be an evil act and would—if he were responsible for it—imply that he was *already* evil. It follows that the evil of a person *must* precede the act of making himself evil. Therefore this individual cannot ultimately be the responsible source of his own evil. Then who is? It cannot be Satan, for the same argument would apply to him. It must be God, for he created everything. Therefore God is ultimately responsible for all evil.

XIV. God and Jesus

The New Testament account of Jesus frequently makes magnificent and exaggerated claims about him and then later admits, although indirectly, that they are false. A few examples should suffice. Consider first the Virgin Birth. Both of Jesus's parents were informed by angels before his birth that he was the Son of God (Matt. 1:20; Luke 1:26-35). If both Joseph and Mary knew Jesus was so exceptional, they should not have been surprised at his extraordinary behavior. Yet in Luke 2:41-50, Joseph and Mary were "amazed" when the twelve-year-old Jesus was discussing religion with the rabbis in the temple. And when Jesus's parents criticized him for wandering off from them, Jesus "said unto them, How is it that ye sought me? Wist ye not that I must be about my Father's business? *And they understood not the saying which he spake unto them.*" Now if angels had appeared to them to announce Jesus as the Son of God, Joseph and Mary would hardly have had trouble understanding what their son meant by his "Father's business."

We are told that John the Baptist enthusiastically recognized Jesus as the Son of God at the beginning of Jesus's ministry (John 1:25-34). Note: "The next day John seeth Jesus coming unto him, and saith, Behold the Lamb of God, which taketh away the sin of the world. . . . I saw and bare record that this is the Son of God" (John 1:29-34). After this explicit recognition by John the Baptist Jesus goes on to perform many "works" (John 2:1-2; 2:14-16; 2:23) and then starts baptizing (John 3:22). "And John also was baptizing in Enon. . . . For John was not yet cast into prison" (John 3:23-24). "Now when John had heard in the prison the works of Christ, he sent two of his disciples, and said unto him, Art thou he that should come or do we look for another?" (Matt. 11:2-3; Luke 7:18-22). Thus we are told that John the Baptist was so impressed by his face to face meeting with Jesus that he positively declared Jesus the Son of God . . . and later, on the basis of rumors of Jesus's "works," he began to suspect that *possibly* Jesus was the Son of God.

Jesus is supposed to have worked miracles. Now when the disciples were told of Jesus's resurrection, at first they did not believe it. They believed the stories to be "idle tales" (Luke 24:11; Mark 16:11-14). And one of Jesus's disciples would not believe even after he had seen Jesus— not until he had touched Jesus (John 20:25-27). Obviously nobody would have found the resurrection so hard to believe if Jesus had performed any of the miracles these disciples are said to have witnessed. They should have been prepared by his past acts to believe anything. Could they have seen him walk on water and create loaves and fishes out of nowhere and raise the dead and yet *doubt* a report that he had returned to life?

We are told in Matthew 28:1-15 that the soldiers who were guarding Jesus's tomb became extremely frightened when an angel descended from heaven and announced the resurrection. But the soldiers were nonetheless so unimpressed that they allowed themselves to be bribed by the Jewish priests to keep quiet about it and instead claim that Jesus's disciples came and stole his body while they were asleep. How could the soldiers have the courage to tell lies about someone whom they had just witnessed with their own eyes to be dangerously supernatural? Their rather bored and matter-of—fact reaction to the wonders they supposedly witnessed fits right in with the unbelief of the disciples when told of Jesus's resurrection.

As for the resurrection, it can be shown to be unlikely with evidence derived from the New Testament. The very fact that a supposedly dead man was seen alive after his reported death is an indication that he was never dead in the first place. Crucifixion was a slow death. Pilate expressed surprise that Jesus was dead so soon (Mark 15:44). Jesus was taken down from the cross much sooner than he would otherwise have been, because it was the beginning of the Sabbath, during which no crucifixion was permitted (John 19:31). The soldiers broke the legs of the two thieves who were crucified with Jesus, but because they believed Jesus was dead already, they did not break his legs (John 19:32-33). Obviously the two thieves were still alive since it was thought necessary to break their legs. Why should Jesus have died so much sooner than the two thieves—so much so that Pilate was actually surprised? Jesus was not buried deep in the ground by his enemies. Instead he was put into a cave tomb prepared for one of his followers, Joseph of Arimathea. There was only a rock rolled against it to block the entrance—presumably not cutting off much air (Matt. 27:57-60). Now this Joseph of Arimathea was a rich man (Matt. 27:57), and rich men have been known to engage in bribery. It is therefore quite possible that the soldiers who crucified Jesus were bribed not to be too thorough in ensuring that he was dead. What other reason is there for not breaking his legs? Why was the report of Jesus's quick death so surprising to Pilate? If Jesus's head had been cut off or his body had been burned to ashes, or even had his legs been broken like those of the two thieves, his reappearance would have been very impressive. But all that happened to him was that he hung for a few hours on a cross with nails in his hands, and sustained a spear wound in his side which, for all we are told to the contrary, may have been slight. As for Joseph, he would not be likely to tell anyone at all that he had bribed the soldiers. He would naturally wish to avoid trouble.

Theists may object that it is nowhere recorded that Joseph was observed bribing soldiers and that therefore this theory is based on mere assumption. But it is nowhere recorded that God was observed raising Jesus from the dead. The theistic theory is also based on mere assumption. Moreover, my theory accounts for more facts. Consider that, in almost every post-resurrection appearance, Jesus's disciples had difficulty recognizing him (John 20: 14-15; Luke 24:16; Mark 16:12; Matthew 28:17). It appears Jesus was disguised in order to avoid recapture. Why did he avoid appearing to his enemies? He appeared only to his disciples in rooms with locked doors or on out-of-the-way mountains. Jesus seems to have lacked confidence that his being alive was due to an actual resurrection; and he seems to have felt that he might not be so lucky next time if he were to be crucified for a second time.

XV. God and the Meaning of Life

We have now come nearly to the end of a frank and often contentious survey of theism. A final question may be asked by the theist: "If there is no God, then what is the meaning of life?"

It is true that, for the atheist, God's supposed desires and plans are no more significant than the possibility of being run over by Santa Claus or being kidnapped by the tooth fairy. But this fact does not deprive life of meaning any more than the realization that Santa Claus does not exist deprives gift-giving of its significance. Atheism could only undermine inquiry into the meaning of life if that question presupposed a theistic answer. For example, if it is interpreted to mean "Why are we here?", then of course the atheist can give no answer. But this inability results from the fact that the question presupposes the existence of an intelligent being who put us here for a reason. It is foolish to believe that the atheist's inability to answer such a question demonstrates some inherent limitation of his position. The question resembles: "When did you cease being a Communist?" This last question presupposes that the person being addressed was once a Communist. If he was never a Communist, then of course he cannot answer the question.[52]

In conclusion, allow me to offer a brief summary of what has been accomplished. First, we have shown that it is up to the theist to prove his position. The theist offers us an explanation of various facts of existence and he must give us reasons for accepting that explanation. Second, we have shown that the theist's reasoning is faulty and therefore cannot support his claims. Our ignorance of alternative explanations does not justify acceptance of the theistic explanation, because ignorance does not justify explanations—only knowledge does. The various traditional arguments provide no justification for belief in God's existence largely because they *presuppose* his existence. Our culture has a tradition of theism. Theistic assumptions are often unconsciously adopted and find their way into the premises of arguments for God's existence. But they have no place there. We cannot merely assume what we are proposing to prove. We must start with undisputed premises. But if we do so, it is impossible to prove God's existence. Finally, we have shown that there is good evidence against the existence of God, whether considered in a general way as a good Creator or more specifically as the Christian God. On the question of the existence of God, the only reasonable position is atheism.

NOTES

1. Norwood Russell Hanson, *What I Do Not Believe* (Dordrecht: D. Reidel, 1971), p. 310.

2. Ibid., p. 322.

3. J. C. A. Gaskin, "The Design Argument: Hume's Critique of Poor Reason," *Religious Studies,* XII (1976), p. 342.

4. Gilbert Fulmer, "The Concept of the Supernatural," *Analysis,* XXXVII (1977), pp. 113-114.

5. R. T. Hinton, "God and the Possibility of Science" *Sophia,* XII (1973), pp. 25-29.

6. R. G. Swinburne, "The Argument From Design," *Philosophy,* XXXXIII (1068), pp. 207-212.

7. Gary Doore, "The Argument From Design: Some Better Reasons For Agreeing With Hume," *Religious Studies,* XVI, (1980), pp. 149-150.

8. William E. Kennick, "On Proving That God Exists," in Sidney Hook (ed.), *Religious Experience and Truth* (New York: New York University Press, 1961), pp. 261-269.

9. Wallace I. Matson, *The Existence of God* (Ithaca: Cornell University Press, 1965), p. 129.

10. Ibid., p. 130.

11. W. T. Stace, *The Nature of the World* (New York: Greenwood Press, 1969), p. 247.

12. Chapman Cohen, *Theism or Atheism* (London: The Pioneer Press, 1921), pp. 73-74.

13. Leon Pearl, *Four Philosophical Problems* (New York: Harper and Row, 1963), pp. 41-42.

14. Chapman Cohen, *Theism or Atheism*, pp. 82-83.

15. Ronald J. Glass, "Taylor's Argument From Design," *The Personalist*, LIV (1973), p. 96.

16. Richard Taylor, *Metaphysics* (Englewood Cliffs: Prentice-Hall, 1963), pp. 96-102.

17. Walter H. O'Briant, "A New Argument From Design?" *Sophia*, V (1966), pp. 32-34.

18. David Hume, *Dialogues Concerning Natural Religion* (New York: Hafner, 1948), pp. 32-35.

19. W. T. Stace, *Religion and the Modern Mind* (Philadelphia: J. B. Lippincott, 1952), pp. 79-80.

20. A. J. Ayer, *Metaphysics and Common Sense* (San Francisco: Freeman, Cooper and Co., 1970), pp. 106-110.

21. Wallace I. Matson, *The Existence of God*, pp. 117-118.

22. W. D. Hudson, *A Philosophical Approach to Religior* (London: Macmillan, 1974), p. 49.

23. John Morreall, "God As Self-Explanatory," *Philosophical Quarterly*, XXX (1980), pp. 208-209.

24. Carolyn Morillo, "The Logic of Arguments from Contingency," *Philosophy and Phenomenological Research*, XXXVII (1977), pp. 412-413.

25. Ibid., p. 413.

26. William E. Kennick, "On Proving That God Exists," pp. 261-269.

27. Paul Edwards, "The Cosmological Argument," in Baruch Brody (ed.), *Readings in the Philosophy of Religion* (Englewood Cliffs: Prentice-Hall, 1974), p. 73.

28. Wallace I. Matson, *The Existence of God*, p. 60.

29. St. Anselm, *St. Anselm: Basic Writings,* trans. by S. N. Deane (La Salle: Open Court, 1961), p. 8.

30. W. D. Hudson, *A Philosophical Approach to Religion,* op. cit., p. 31.

31. C. J. Ducasse, *A Philosophical Scrutiny of Religion* (New York: Ronald Press, 1953), p. 273.

32. P. S. Wadia, "Miracles and Common Understanding," *Philosophical Quarterly,* XXVII (1976), pp. 78-81.

33. Alastair McKinnon, "Miracle and Paradox," *American Philosophical Quarterly* IV (1967), pp. 308-314.

34. R. G. Swinburne, *The Concept of Miracle* (New York: Macmillan, 1972), pp. 45-50.

35. George D. Chryssides, "Miracles and Agents," *Religious Studies,* XI (1976), pp. 321-323.

36. David Hume, "Of Miracles," in Baruch Brody, op. cit., pp. 439-442.

37. J. J. MacIntosh, "Belief-In," *Mind,* LXXIX (1970), p. 403.

38. Michael Scriven, *Primary Philosophy* (New York: McGraw-Hill, 1966), pp. 136-137.

39. Gilbert Fulmer, "The Concept of the Supernatural," p. 114.

40. Thomas C. Mayberry, "Standards and Criteria," *Mind,* LXXXI (1972), pp. 87-91.

41. Plato, *Euthyphro,* found in Baruch Brody (ed.), *Readings in the Philosophy of Religion,* pp. 562-564.

42. Ronald W. Hepburn, *Christianity and Paradox* (London: Watts, 1958), pp. 130-131.

43. Ibid., p. 139.

44. Walter Kaufmann, *Critique of Religion and Philosophy* (New York: Harper and Brothers, 1958), p. 83.

45. Marvin Zimmerman, "Faith, Hope and Clarity," in Sidney Hook (ed.), op. cit., pp. 187-190.

46. Blaise Pascal, *Pensées* (London: Dent, 1931), p. 66.

47. Steven M. Cahn, "Cacodaemony," *Analysis* XXXVII (1967), pp. 69-73.

48. Michael Martin, "A Disproof of God's Existence," *Darshana International,* (1970), pp. 40-45.

49. Ibid., p. 44.

50. Walter Kaufmann, *Critique of Religion and Philosophy,* p. 146.

51. Gertrude Ezorsky, "The Ethics of Punishment," in Gertrude Ezorsky (ed.), *Philosophical Perspectives on Punishment* (Albany: State University of New York Press, 1972), pp. xxiv-xxvi.

52. Jerome Shaffer, *Reality, Knowledge and Value* (New York: Random House, 1971), pp. 104-105.

BIBLIOGRAPHY

Anselm, St. *St. Anselm: Basic Writings.* Trans. by S. N. Deane.
La Salle: Open Court, 1961.

Ayer, A. J. *Metaphysics and Common Sense.* San Francisco:
Freeman, Cooper and Co., 1970.

Cahn, Steven. "Cacodamony." *Analysis,* XXXVII (1977), pp. 69–
73.

*Chrysiddes, George D. "Miracles and Agents." Religious Stud-
ies,* XI (1976), pp. 319–327.

Cohen, Chapman, *Theism or Atheism.* London: The Pioneer
Press, 1921.

Doore, Gary. "The Argument From Design: Some Better Reasons for Agreeing With Hume." *Religious Studies,* XVI (1980),
pp. 142–158.

Ducasse, C. J. *A Philosophical Scrutiny of Religion.* New York:
Ronald Press, 1953.

Edwards, Paul. "The Cosmological Argument." *Readings in the
Philosophy of Religion,* edited by Baruch Brody. Englewood-
Cliffs: Prentice-Hall, 1974.

Ezorsky, Gertrude. "The Ethics of Punishment." *Philosophical
Perspectives on Punishment,* edited by Gertrude Ezorsky.
Albany: State University of New York Press, 1972.

Fulmer, Gilbert. "The Concept of the Supernatural." *Analysis,* XXXVII (1977), pp. 113–116.

Gaskin, J. C. A. "The Design Argument: Hume's Critique of Poor Reason." *Religious Studies,* XII (1976), pp. 332–345.

Glass, Ronald J. "Taylor's Argument From Design." *The Personalist,* LIV (1973), pp. 94–99.

Hanson, Norwood Russell. *What I Do Not Believe.* Dordrecht: D. Reidl, 1971.

Hepburn, Ronald W. *Christianity and Paradox.* London: Watts, 1958.

Hinton, R. T. "God and the Possibility of Science." *Sophia,* XII (1973), pp. 25–29.

Hudson, W. D. *A Philosophical Approach to Religion.* London: Macmillan, 1974.

Hume, David. *Dialogues Concerning Natural Religion.* New York: Hafner, 1948.

Kaufmann, Walter. *Critique of Religion and Philosophy.* New York: Harper and Brothers, 1958.

MacIntosh, J. J. "Belief-In." *Mind,* LXXIX (1970), pp. 395–407.

McKinnon, Alastair. "Miracle and Paradox." *American Philosophical Quarterly,* IV (1967), pp. 308–314.

Martin, Michael. "A Disproof of God's Existence." *Darshana International,* IV (1970), pp. 40–45.

Matson, Wallace I. *The Existence of God.* Ithaca: Cornell University Press, 1965.

Mayberry, Thomas. "Standards and Criteria." *Mind,* LXXXI (1972), pp. 87–91.

Morillo, Carolyn. "The Logic of Arguments From Contingency." *Philosophy and Phenomenological Research,* XXXVII (1977), pp. 408–417.

Morreall, John. "God As Self-Explanatory." *Philosophical Quarterly,* XXX (1980), pp. 206–214.

O'Briant, Walter H. "A New Argument From Design?" *Sophia,* V (1966), pp. 30–34.

Pascal, Blaise. *Pensées.* London: Dent, 1931.

Pearl, Leon. *Four Philosophical Problems.* New York: Harper and Row, 1963.

Scriven, Michael. *Primary Philosophy.* New York: McGraw-Hill, 1966.

Shaffer, Jerome. *Reality, Knowledge and Value.* New York: Random House, 1971.

Stace, W. T. *The Nature of the World.* New York: Greenwood Press, 1969.

Stace, W. T. *Religion and the Modern Mind.* Philadelphia: J. B. Lippincott, 1952.

Swinburne, R. G. "The Argument From Design." *Philosophy,* XXXXIII (1968), pp. 202–215.

Swinburne, R. G. *The Concept of Miracle.* New York: Macmillan, 1972.

Taylor, Richard. *Metaphysics.* Englewood Cliffs: Prentice-Hall, 1963.

Wadia, P. S. "Miracles and Common Understanding." *Philosophical Quarterly,* XXVII (1976), pp. 69–81.

Zimmerman, Marvin. "Faith, Hope and Clarity." *Religious Experience and Truth,* edited by Sidney Hook. New York: New York University Press, 1961.

SUGGESTED READING LIST

Anderson, John. "Design." *Australasian Journal of Philosophy*, XIII (1935), pp. 241-256.

Flew, Antony. *God and Philosophy*. New York: Harcourt, Brace and World, 1969.

Kenny, Anthony. *The Five Ways*. New York: Schocken Books, 1969.

Laird, John. *Theism and Cosmology*. Freeport: Books For Libraries Press, 1969.

Martin, C. B. *Religious Belief*. Ithaca: Cornell University Press, 1959.

McCloskey, H. J. "God and Evil." *Philosophical Quarterly*, X (1960), pp. 97-114.

Mellor, D. H. "God and Probability." *Religious Studies*, V (1969), pp. 223-234.

Olding, A. "The Argument From Design—A Reply to R. G. Swinburne." *Religious Studies*, VII (1971), pp. 361-373.

Olding, A. "Design—A Further Reply to R. G. Swinburne," *Religious Studies*, IX (1973), pp. 229-232.

Plantinga, Alvin. *God and Other Minds*. Ithaca: Cornell University Press, 1967.

Puccetti, Roland. "The Concept of God." *Philosophical Quarterly,* XV (1964), pp. 227–245.

Puccetti, Roland. "The Loving God." *Religious Studies,* II (1966), pp. 255–268.

Richman, Robert J. "Plantinga, God and (Yet) Other Minds." *Australasian Journal of Philosophy,* L (1972), pp. 40–55.

Salmon, Wesley C. "Religion and Science: A New Look at Hume's *Dialogues.*" *Philosophical Studies,* XXXIII (1978), pp. 143–176.

Smith, George H. *Atheism: The Case Against God.* Buffalo: Prometheus Books, 1979.

Warren, Thomas B., and Flew, Antony. *The Warren-Flew Debate on the Existence of God.* Jonesboro: National Christian Press, 1977.

Warren, Thomas B., and Matson, Wallace I. *The Warren-Matson Debate on the Existence of God.* Jonesboro: National Christian Press, 1979.